Tales fr Joe Zone

Sixteen Entertaining Stories

Joe B. Stallings, Jr.

outskirts
press

Contents

Introduction

I do break several *rules* of writing. One, don't use a big word when a simple word will do. I enjoy learning new words and feel cheated if I don't have to look up at least one word when reading a short story. I am confident you will need a dictionary at times while reading my stories. Also, I use archaic words. And there is a drink I reference in several stories that you will think I have misspelled—I haven't. Two, don't leave things open-ended. I don't explain everything, as I think it's important for people to use their imaginations. That's one reason movies will never be as good as books, usually. Three, writers aren't supposed to act like a know-it-all. I'm not, but I do like to sprinkle facts—often obscure—into my stories. There are several instances when I have referenced the same person, book, or facts in more than one story as I had not envisioned publishing the stories together when I started writing. Four, I occasionally use the word *that*—a relative pronoun—when it is not necessary. Why? Two reasons. It sounds better to me. And if you diagram a sentence, you include *that,* even if it's not written. And finally, five, in one of my stories, "The News Not Printed," I followed the guidelines in the *Associated Press Stylebook* and not the *Chicago Manual of Style.*

My stories are not meant to disparage any person, sex,

organization, association, belief, or anything at all. They are meant to be entertaining. As a famous author once told an English teacher whose students were reading his novel, *"Sometimes a story is just a story."*

1

Blackmail

For more than twenty years I had earned a living from one job. I concocted the idea in law school. After I graduated and passed the bar, I launched my career in blackmail. The punishment for blackmail in the state where I lived was minor: one year in prison and a ten-thousand-dollar fine, max. If no interstate commerce or government officials were involved, the federal government couldn't prosecute, which meant additional charges for extortion and larceny were off the table. State prosecutors loathed those cases because they required cooperation from the victim, which was difficult—usually impossible—to obtain.

No blackmail case I'd worked on had imploded—until now. The art of blackmail is learned by doing. There is no other way. You can't anticipate everything, so you have to be flexible, ready to change directions at a moment's notice without flinching. And you always have to be ready to walk away. I did back out once, at the last minute. I had met Sofia Gustafsson for the exchange—money for the documents. During our conversation, I learned that she was the great-granddaughter of Sofia Kovalevskaya, a woman I greatly admire. Before she was nine years old she became interested in math because her bedroom was wallpapered with her father's calculus notes. She overcame many obstacles to become, among other things, the first woman to obtain a doctorate in mathematics in 1874. Perhaps the most famous professional woman in the world prior to the twentieth century. She died at forty-one. I explained my feelings to the younger Sofia and left empty-handed—no money and no blackmail material.

I never asked the gifters for more than they could easily afford. They were not victims. According to the law, a victim is someone who is injured or harmed. Considering the gifters' income and net worth, my $250,000 gift request was trivial. And after I got the money, I turned over all my blackmail material, never to see them again. I never chose gifters who lived where I did; it would have been embarrassing to bump shopping carts at the Piggly Wiggly.

Blackmail is time consuming. A single operation could take years from start to finish. Finding a suitable gifter took the most time. Just when you thought you'd found one, your hopes were dashed. The person's transgressions were already on YouTube or Facebook or Twitter. Transgressions that would have been repugnant twenty years ago scarcely cause a reaction now.

I used an assortment of methods to find gifters. I had several private eyes in the state's largest city on retainer, and I told them I was an online gossip columnist—freelance—working under a nom de plume. I paid them a small fee in exchange for a monthly letter they sent to a post office box with whatever tidbits they'd uncovered. If I used their information, I paid them a ten-thousand-dollar bonus. As a precaution, I enlisted a courier to pick up the mail from my PO box and send it to a secondary box at another location.

I got to know domestic household staff, visited the watering holes of the well-to-do, crashed high-society parties, and surfed the web. My sources were endless.

I lived alone in a modest neighborhood and rented space in a suburban office complex for my work. My neighbors were acquaintances, not friends, and they believed I was a business consultant. Because of my modest lifestyle and savings, I could, most likely, live out the remainder of my life without working in the traditional sense, but I liked my work. I liked the challenge. And I paid taxes on all my earnings, which I labeled "consulting income" on my tax return. Not reporting it was not an option. If the IRS could show that your lifestyle was above your reported income, you were going to prison irrespective of how the money was earned. Because fraudulent tax returns would've been the easiest way for the government to catch me, I wasn't taking any chances.

There were downsides to my vocation. I would've liked to have gotten married and had a family, but I didn't think it was safe; although, I did date occasionally. I was in love once. I came close to telling Clair what I did for a living and asking her to marry me. Why I didn't is a story in itself. It simply wasn't a good idea for me to get too close to anyone.

There were substantial upsides to the job as well. I could work when, where, how, and as much or as little as I wanted. That benefit was priceless.

I had been looking for a gifter for two years when I received an envelope from one of my private eyes. A note and CD were enclosed. The CD contained photos of hundreds of documents. The note read:

My client, for personal reasons that she did not elaborate, wanted photos of all the documents in her husband's safe. She gave me the safe's combination and turned off the alarm systems on a day the family and household staff were gone. I encountered no problems while taking the photos. Before I could arrange to give this CD to the client, she called me to say that issues had been resolved and she didn't need the photos. Since I have been paid in full, I have no use for them.

That was different. Usually I received a handwritten note, maybe a photo or two, but never a CD with hundreds of documents. Reviewing that material would take a while. First, I studied just enough from the CD to determine who the people were—Milton and Dora Hightower. Before I examined the CD in detail, I researched elsewhere: online, several years of the local paper, Freedom-of-Information-Act documents, and more. I also got myself hired as one of the Hightowers' gardeners. I needed to get some perspective on the gifter, if possible, while staying in the background. Any nuance could prove vital. I was rarely in the house—just the kitchen a few times. I never saw Mr. Hightower, and I saw Mrs. Hightower only a couple of times from a distance.

After eight months of research and planning, I believed I had my gifter. The documents on the CD could get Milton Hightower guaranteed jail time. He was seventy and a recluse. I could find only two older pictures of him, both very grainy. He had immigrated to the United States from France twenty years earlier. He'd been living in Paris. I couldn't find out where he had lived before Paris, but I suspected Ireland. He'd earned his millions before coming to this country. From the information in his safe and implications from other sources, which were scarce, I hypothesized that he'd been a gunrunner for the Irish Republican Army (IRA) and had been skimming. Considering how long he'd been doing it, the scale of weapons, and the amount of money involved, I expected he would get a hefty sentence. He might have been hiding from the IRA too, which would explain his hermetic behavior. Although I found no evidence of violent acts, I suspected the chances were slim that a gunrunner for the IRA would not have *taken care of* someone. I never blackmailed anyone with violent tendencies; it wasn't worth the risk, and Milton appeared to be in that category.

Milton's wife, Dora, was forty-seven, born and raised in the States. She'd married Milton shortly after his arrival in this country. She was a wealthy heiress, the great-granddaughter of a chemical company founder. She had a doctorate in psychology from Duke and was wealthy in her own right—a good bit wealthier than Milton. Often several of the local dress shops and beauty salons ran slick ads in the local city magazine with Dora modeling outfits or hairstyles, so I had plenty of pictures of her posted on my office wall. Perhaps because of her coquettish smile, I'd pinned up more than I needed.

Although I decided not to blackmail Milton, at least not directly, I did decide to blackmail Dora for several reasons. First, I was confident that paying me only $250,000 would not even be the slightest nuisance. Second, it was clear that Dora was an independent woman who made her own decisions in financial matters. Third, considering her gregarious nature and status in the community, she'd want to avoid a family scandal. And fourth, because of what I'd gathered about their relationship, I was confident that she would never tell Milton.

I called Dora to arrange the exchange. I told her what I had, what I knew, and what I wanted. I normally picked a dive for the exchange.

"Meet me at Bert's Place on Fifth Avenue at ten thirty Thursday morning," I told her.

"That won't do," she replied. "Harolday's Café on the river. You know it—ten miles out of town on the old north-south highway. Ten thirty is fine."

No one had tried to change the meeting place before. I knew of Harolday's Café. I relished the place and ate there once a month. It was a typical diner built in the fifties—long and narrow, lots of windows, bright, airy, clean, friendly staff, and it always had an excellent Health Department rating. And the times I had been to Harolday's, it only had a few customers.

"Why there?"

"I like it."

"Okay." Since I liked the place too and with few customers, I didn't see a problem.

"I'll see you then."

I arrived at Harolday's Café at ten and ordered breakfast. I was the only customer. Dora Hightower arrived three minutes later and stopped at the counter.

"Susie, I'll have what the gentleman is having."

"What Nate is having?"

"Nate . . . yes, what Nate is having." Then she opened her purse and placed some money on the counter. "Keep the change."

"Thanks, Mrs. Hightower."

Dora turned toward me and, unperturbed, joined me at my booth. Her curly, jet-black hair fell to her shoulders. She wore a lime-green dress with quarter-sized white polka dots and lime-green high heels. Her face wore a bright smile, as if she were looking forward to meeting me.

"Hi," she said and held out her hand.

"Hi," I replied and shook her hand.

"The gloves aren't necessary."

I smiled. "You ordered breakfast?"

"Why not? You did. We might as well enjoy breakfast first."

"Why not indeed. Please, have a seat."

She sat down next to me rather than across. We engaged in small talk, our faces seemingly inches apart, until the food arrived. Her eyes were alluring, and her eye shadow was subtle. She wore eyeliner thicker on the outside of her eyes, and her eyelashes featured a touch of mascara. Her makeup collaborated to accentuate her green eyes. After we finished eating, Susie came over and took our plates. Since Mrs. Hightower was being cute with me, I decided to be cute right back.

"So, Mrs. Hightower, your eye shadow, I notice you apply it over primer."

She burst out laughing. "Nate, you're delightful. This is going to be a lot more fun than I imagined. But why are you blackmailing me? It's my husband with the secrets."

I could tell by the look in her eyes and the way the corner of her mouth turned up slightly that she knew the answer.

"Dr. Hightower, you're a smart woman—a degree in philosophy from City College of New York, an MBA from Harvard, and a doctorate in psychology from Duke. I'm sure you know why. I assume the money is in your briefcase."

"Nate, about the amount—$250,000—that won't work for me. Let's make it $500,000," she said without sarcasm.

Something was wrong. Why would a gifter want to pay more?

"Just so we understand each other, Mr. Nate Thomas of 214 Greenwell Drive, $500,000 is the amount I want from *you.* You have more than that in your account at the National City Bank. It's either $500,000 or something . . . something more involved I'll require of you."

Before I could even begin to comprehend what was happening, little black dots—more and more of them—filled my field of vision. Dora Hightower had drugged me.

When I awoke, I was in my own bed. I could barely move my legs. My arms weren't much better. Nothing hurt; I just couldn't move.

Dora pranced in. "You're awake, good. I met your neighbor, Sandra. I introduced myself and told her I was an old friend of yours."

"You told her your real name?"

"Why not?"

That was spooky, her broadcasting her identity. Dora pulled up a chair and sat by my bed.

"Nate, I'll give you five options. You'll get one option at a time to choose or refuse. Refuse an option and you lose it. If you refuse the first four, the last one will be required. I've already given you your first option: pay me $500,000. Once you choose an option, that's it. You'll never know what the other options were. But that mirrors life, doesn't it, having to make decisions under conditions of uncertainty? It's poker, not chess.

"I'm giving you an edge here, Nate. Some of your options will be less arduous than others. As odd as it sounds, you may like some of the options."

Like some of the options? What the heck? I was utterly bewildered. Perhaps I was dreaming; I couldn't fathom how this setup made any sense.

"When the drug wears off—in about an hour—I'm sure we'll have no trouble doing business. I know you make a living off blackmail."

With that she handed me a stack of about ten pictures. The first half were pictures of the blackmail material that I once had on other people but that I no longer possessed. How could she have those? It wasn't possible, unless . . . but that would mean these pictures had been taken . . . that can't be. The remaining pictures were of my wall—my pictures of her.

"I mean you no harm, Nate. If you lash out at me, you'll lose. And you realize that I can wreak more havoc on you than you can on me. You want to go after Milton? Go ahead. That's enough business for now. I'll fix us lunch, including macaroni and cheese like your grandmother made with cheese that's baked in a casserole pan with spaghetti noodles and not soupy. Why don't we eat on the patio? It's such a nice day. After lunch we'll get down to business."

Dora left the room.

Whoa! That was bizarre. How did she know so much about me? Why would she want money from me? And what were the options she talked about? I did feel confident about one thing: I wasn't going to outsmart her.

My first option was to pay her $500,000. She was right—I did have that much in my savings account at the National City Bank. I could pay her and be done. I'd still have some money, and I'd be okay for a while. Yet I expected my blackmailing days would be over.

Still, I was inclined to pass. I wanted to know my next option. Call it curiosity. If the option was worse, I'd pass on that one too. Dora said I may *like* some of my options. But does *like* mean pleasant, or does it mean bearable? I wasn't interested in bearable. After all, giving her $500,000 was bearable. My chance of picking the best option would be pure luck.

Dora returned an hour later. I could move my arms and

legs, but only a little. She helped me to the patio. Neither of us spoke while we were eating. She was right; the macaroni and cheese was like my grandmother made. When she finished her last bite, I started my questioning.

"Why are you doing this? You have money."

"Maybe I don't want money," she said playfully, and she flashed a wide smile and raised her eyebrows.

"How many options are pleasant?"

"Impossible for me to know. I don't know you *that* well."

"Educated guess."

She thought for a moment as she gazed into the distance. "To me they're all more pleasant than your first one, but they're very different kinds of options. It's not an apples-to-apples comparison. What you find pleasant today, you might not find pleasant tomorrow—or in ten years."

Ten years! What did that mean? What could that mean? "How much time will I have to decide on each option?"

"With some, perhaps a few weeks, but with others, maybe a few hours."

"Why the difference?"

"Depends on my mood and how much fun we're having."

Fun? "How long do I have for my first option?"

"I'll give you a week, but I expect you've already decided."

"What have I decided?"

"You're not going to take it. I imagine you're curious anent your other options. And maybe, just maybe, for that reason I might help you. I might save your best option—at least to me—for last. Wouldn't that be considerate?"

"You're blackmailing me, and you're trying to be considerate?"

"Yes."

I wasn't sure that helped me.

"Let's move on. What's my second option?"

"You work for my husband for one year. He'll hire you on my recommendation, and you'll be paid a million, off the books, tax-free."

"What will I do for your husband?"

"Whatever he asks."

"What if your husband won't pay me a million?"

"I'll make up the shortfall."

"I might have to kill someone?"

Dora didn't flinch. "You might only have to play chess with him on Friday nights or wash the limo every other Thursday."

"How much time do I have to decide?"

"A week, but I expect you've already made up your mind, considering what you know about Milton."

One million tax-free for playing chess for a year, What could be better? But I couldn't take the chance. "I'll pass. Third option?"

"Get your license to practice law reinstated—"

"But I'd need to—"

"I know what you'd need to do. Let me finish. Once you're reinstated, I'll have you appointed as a judge. Then I'll need a favor—only one—a favor on a ruling. I promise you this: the ruling will not bother your conscience."

I had questions that I knew I shouldn't ask: What was the case? How did she have the power to have me appointed as a judge? How could she know the matter in question would be assigned to me? But I did ask, "What if you're wrong about my conscience?"

"I'll acknowledge that I could be wrong—uncertainty again. But I don't think so."

"Will you pay me?"

"No, but you get to keep your $500,000."

That option could work. My mind was racing. What's the worst that could happen—letting someone off who was guilty of a horrendous crime? I didn't consider that scenario likely, but I couldn't know.

"It would take me three months to get reinstated."

"I know."

"How long do I have to make a decision?"

"Three days. But that's enough business; let's do the dishes. I'll wash, you dry."

After Dora washed the last dish, she left the kitchen while I continued drying. When I finished, I wandered into the den and found a note. It read:

Nate,

I'll be back Thursday—lunch, my treat. I'll bring something you'll enjoy. Your dirty clothes are clean and in the laundry room. The towels are in the dryer. Your home office could use some paint. I suggest light green for an accent wall—the wall with the light switch. I can pick the color and do the painting or recommend someone if you're afraid of me doing it. Oh yes, I left Alice's Adventures in Wonderland on your bed. Enjoy!

Yours,

Dora

That figured—*Alice's Adventures in Wonderland.*

By lunchtime Thursday I hadn't made a decision. Dora arrived with French bread and gazpacho—my mother's recipe and my favorite dish. Nothing surprised me anymore. Dora was wearing a light summer dress, sleeveless, black with small white butterflies, and white sandals. Her lips were highlighted with subtle red lipstick, and her eyes were as beautiful as usual. There was no denying she was attractive.

During lunch and while doing the dishes, we didn't talk shop. Only after sitting to relax on the den's plush sofas did I broach the subject.

"Are you going to ask me if I've decided? Or maybe you can save me some time, and tell me what I'll decide."

"If I decided for you and you liked the option, you'd think you were lucky. If you didn't like the option, you'd blame me."

"Does that matter?"

"It does, and it doesn't. Can you make sense out of nonsense? Of course you can. People do all the time. I have two tickets to the symphony tomorrow night. I'll pick you up at seven."

I thought, *You've got to be kidding*, but then— "What are they playing?"

"Brahms's Fourth Symphony and Raff's Fourth Symphony."

"Brahms's Fourth Symphony; my favorite. Why am I not surprised? But Raff? They never play Raff."

"They are."

"Why?"

"Why not?"

"But they never play Raff."

"You don't want them to?"

"No, that's not it. I love Raff's Fourth Symphony."

"Then what are you going on for? If something is random, is there a reason for it? Maybe you want to believe there is. Or maybe a patron arranged for a special contribution if that symphony was played."

"Won't Milton object if you take me to the symphony?"

"No."

"Why not? What if someone sees us—a friend or a gossip columnist?"

"He doesn't have friends, and he never reads gossip columns."

"How do I know that's true . . . never . . . never mind."

A slight grimace came over Dora's face at my question, but it dissipated with my "never mind."

With our discussion finished, we played chess and went bowling. We laughed, we smiled, and we told jokes. We had ordinary conversations, as if we were on a first date. What is your favorite book, movie, TV show? Mine: *A Gentleman in Moscow, The Best Years of Our Lives, Sherlock.* Hers: *The Rules of Civility, Tall in the Saddle, Little House on the Prairie.* The conversation featured unusual comments throughout. Why was Bob Dylan given the Nobel Prize for literature? Surely the only picture in Immanuel Kant's house wasn't of Jean-Jacques Rousseau, someone people often mistake for a philosopher. Dora was clearly enjoying herself and so was I. So much so, that I almost forgot she was blackmailing me.

The next evening, rather than driving herself in the Lexus, she arrived at seven in a limousine. The chauffeur was Maranda. I'd seen her occasionally when I worked as a gardener. If she remembered me, she didn't let on.

Brahms and Raff were terrific. And naturally, Dora knew many of the people there. Most remarked that it was good to see she wasn't alone. Dora introduced me by my real name— which surprised me—as a friend who also loved classical music. Her friends were quite pleasant.

When Dora dropped me off after the symphony, she walked me to the door and gave me a brief hug.

"I had a good time. I'll pick you up in the morning at eight for a breakfast 'nic.'"

"Breakfast 'nic'?"

"Yes. Breakfast picnic."

"Okay." After all, no harm had come to me, and I was enjoying myself in spite of the odd situation.

The next day, she picked me up in the Lexus, and we drove to a mostly deserted park on the outskirts of town. Dora retrieved a picnic basket from the back seat, and we found a spot on the grass to spread a large blanket. The park was circular with a wide sidewalk around the perimeter. Beyond the sidewalk were assorted playgrounds and a line of trees. A few people were walking their dogs, and several mothers were there with their children. One woman and her daughter, around age twelve, were enjoying a swing set not far from us. The temperature was just right, and Dora was dressed all in pink: shorts, sandals, and a sleeveless top.

I reached over and opened the picnic basket. Inside were chicken biscuits, fruit cups, and coffee prepared exactly how I took it—lots of cream and no sugar.

As we finished breakfast, the tween girl who'd been swinging nearby skipped over and sat next to me. Dora got up with an anguished expression and headed toward the girl's mother.

"Hello," I said, somewhat surprised. "What's your name?"

"Arly."

"Arly . . . that's a pretty name. Is that short for anything?"

"Yes, Arleta, but I like Arly better."

"Where'd your name come from?"

"Ella Raines—that's why she's my favorite actress."

I chuckled and said, "Ella Raines is your favorite actress, but she's . . . oh, I see . . . she was Arly."

"Yep. And just like my mother, her eyes were—"

"Arly!" her mother called. "Come on and finish swinging. It's about time to go."

Since I do believe in coincidences, I didn't give our conversation a second thought at the time.

"I like Ella Raines too, Arly. Enjoy the rest of your day."

At that Arly popped up and ran over to her mother while Dora headed back to our picnic.

"You find a new girlfriend?" Dora asked.

I chuckled at the implication: *new girlfriend.*

"Did you and Arly have a nice talk? You think you'd ever want any?"

"Any what?"

"Children. I'm too old but you're not."

I turned to watch Arly play, unable to answer the question.

"Well, Arly certainly is adorable," I said.

We lay on the blanket next to each other, gazing at the sky. It was bright blue, and a gentle breeze was blowing. A few minutes went by in silence. Dora gently slid her hand over mine and held it. She looked serene. A few minutes later, she broke the silence.

"Have you decided about option three?"

"I'm going to turn it down."

"Why?"

"I don't believe that my conscience would bother me, but I want to know what my fourth option is."

"You have to be my protégé for one year. Protégé as

portrayed in the movies during the 1930s: Fay Cheney, Carlo, Martha Borden's friend, not protégé as defined in the dictionary. You'll get no compensation, but you'll have free room and board because you'll be living in my house . . . and there would be other fringe benefits."

"You'd be my benefactor?"

"Among other things."

I was a Turner Classics Movies' fan, so I knew the characters she was referring to. The only problem was that I could never tell exactly what those protégés did, although two things were explicit: they went out with their benefactor and learned from their benefactor. Of course, maybe *she* wanted someone killed, though I expected that task would be beyond the requirements of a protégé. This option did appear to be the best yet. Still, I was uncertain.

"How long do I have to decide?"

"How long do you want?"

"A week."

"Okay," she said with a wink.

"I don't suppose you'll list the duties of said protégé?"

"No."

"I suppose I might only have to play chess with you on Friday nights."

"I suppose."

"Or wash the limo every other Thursday."

"Could be."

"Or something disgusting and revolting every day?"

"Maybe. How about dinner Wednesday at La Chateau?"

"Isn't that a fancy place?"

"Yes, suit and tie. I've invited two friends to join us."

"Two friends. I don't suppose I know them."

"Sam and Della Warton."

"I don't. What do they do?"

"A lot of things."

"You know what I mean. What do they do for a living?"

"Sam is the head of the State Patrol, and Della is a professor of philosophy at the university."

"State Patrol, ah . . . I'm not that good at small talk."

"You are. Besides, they want to meet you."

I didn't like the sound of that. "Meet me?"

"Sure. They're glad I'm finally hanging around with someone normal—not Milton."

"Milton's not normal?"

"Not by a long shot. You'll find out."

I didn't like the sound of that either. "How do the Wartons even know about me?"

"I've told them about our dates."

"Dates?"

"Yes. It's not unusual to tell close friends about your dates."

"But you're a married woman." I felt like I was with Alice down the rabbit hole. I hadn't exactly thought of our meetings as dates. *Stop, Nate; you're not going to figure this out.* As I'd initially suspected, I would not be able to outsmart Dora.

"What time will you pick me up?"

"At five. Oh yes—don't concern yourself, but Sam and I will be carrying guns, handguns, concealed of course."

"Excuse me, guns?"

"Yes, the restaurant's in a bad part of town."

"You ever shot anyone?" I asked jokingly.

"On occasion. Well, once. My father, in the leg. Although, technically, I didn't pull the trigger."

"Okay."

"My father collected guns, and he made sure everyone in the family knew how to use them. One day he was teaching me how to use a rifle. It was a bit unwieldy for a six-year-old, and I dropped it. The bullet grazed his calf. I'd been shooting pistols, small ones, since I was five. Dad overestimated my ability to handle a rifle. Do you know how to use a gun?"

"Me . . . yes. Why?"

"Just wondering. You never know when it will come in handy."

I stopped asking questions.

On Wednesday the limo pulled up and Dora climbed out. She rang the bell despite the fact she had a key, a key I had not given her. She was dressed to a T, and everything she wore was deep hunter green—her dress that hung at her knees, her blazer that was trimmed with lace, her sandals, and her small purse. Her hair was lightly streaked with green, and she even wore a green watchband.

"Before I forget, Nate, I have Fleetwood Mac tickets for this weekend, and I thought we could go."

"I didn't know they were still a group. Besides, I don't like concerts."

"It's a reunion tour. Besides, everybody likes concerts."

"I'm not everybody."

We stood at the door, two feet apart, gazing at each other. With her right hand, Dora reached up and gently ran the back of her fingers slowly up and down my cheek. "No, you're not," she said so very softly. "Let's not go."

Dora looked at her hand and quickly dropped it to her side, seemly startled by what she'd done.

When we got to the limo, a man was sitting in the front seat next to Maranda.

Inside the limo, I asked, "Who's the—?"

"Bodyguard."

I closed my eyes and shook my head slightly.

"It'll be okay," Dora said as she reached over and nudged me playfully.

The restaurant could have put the fanciest place in New York City to shame. The furniture was plush, and each table had its own waiter. When the waiters weren't at their tables, they were at the waiters' wall, watching for their customers' signal. I'd never seen such a thing. Finally, a well-dressed couple I could only assume were the Wartons approached our table.

"Nate, pleased to meet you," said Sam. "Dora has said nice things about you, despite the shady business you're in."

We all burst out laughing. What else could I do? Dora smiled sweetly at me.

"Seriously, it's nice to see Dora getting out with a male friend. But I'm surprised someone has the balls."

I had to fight to keep smiling.

"Sam, behave," said Della. "Nate, ignore him. He's a tomfool."

"Well, you know Milton does have a reputation," said Sam.

"Only in your mind," said Dora.

When we sat down, Dora squeezed my knee under the table. I smiled stiffly, excused myself, visited the men's room, and threw up. It was going to take all my energy to make it through this night.

Dora could tell I was uncomfortable and masterfully redirected the conversation any time my jaw began to clench. She knew I'd recently become interested in Roman history and was reading a book about Cicero. As it happened, Sam was a Cicero fanatic. His parents required that he learn Latin, so much of his reading material was Cicero's writings. I found the remainder of our conversation genuinely enjoyable. Dora and Della spent a good bit of time discussing *Alice's Adventures in Wonderland*. It turned out that Della was teaching a class at the university on the logic of *Alice*. Now and then I glimpsed Dora's gun handle in her blazer pocket.

On the way home, Dora asked, "Do you believe in coincidences?"

"Yes, although Sherlock Holmes didn't."

"Does that mean that Sir Arthur didn't?"

"I would assume so."

"That's what Sam's shady business comment was—a coincidence. Have you decided whether you'll take the fourth option?"

"No. I haven't thought about it, as strange as that sounds. Do you know what I'll decide?"

"No idea. I can understand how the decision would be difficult. I'll pick you up Friday morning around eleven. We're going to the mall."

"You need to buy something?"

"No, I want to play a game."

"A game?"

"Yes. I've never played it before. I've read it's popular, and I think it will be fun—with you."

"Will I like it?"

"I don't know. As I've said, I've never played, so I don't know if I'll like it."

"Will it embarrass us?"

"No, not likely."

"Is this what being your protégé would be like—you telling me what to do, not asking me first?"

"Maybe."

"What's the purpose of all these *dates*? To make me believe being your protégé would be fun? Or to mislead me, so I choose it and then have to do terrible things?"

"Don't confuse the two. Blackmail is business; dates are pleasure."

"Of course," I said, totally confused.

When we returned to my house, Dora walked me to the door and gave me a hug and a kiss on the cheek. "See you Friday."

I spent all day Thursday thinking about being Dora's protégé. It didn't seem to be a bad option. But since I didn't know her true motive, I couldn't be sure. I might have to be her lover, or I might have to kill someone—Milton for instance.

And what about Milton? He seemed inconsequential to her. Maybe that's not uncommon for someone married to a recluse. Suppose I had to kill him; would I do it? And if he died, as a recluse, would anyone even notice? I thought about it all day, back and forth. By evening I had no clarity. My decision was more muddled than ever. At least I had time, although I doubted more time would help.

Friday morning Dora looked refreshed, almost glowing. She was wearing white jeans, a white sleeveless top, and white sandals, but there were no green highlights in her hair.

"You look nice, Dora."

"Thank you. Want to see my accessories?"

"Accessories?"

She pulled up the bottom of her jeans, exposing a derringer strapped above her ankle.

"Are we going to need that?"

"You never know," she said with a laugh. "Maybe Milton will show up."

As we were driving, I asked, "What's Milton like?"

"Isn't that a bit personal?"

I laughed for a few seconds; I couldn't help myself. "Personal? His wife is dating me."

"Dating?"

"Your description, not mine."

"How would you describe our relationship?"

"I can't."

"Since you've asked, I'll tell you. I don't like Milton. I don't like him one bit, and I don't know anyone who does. I wish he were gone. But *I* can't kill him. At least I haven't been able to yet."

I was in no position to judge Dora or to think I truly knew her, but still, her comment startled me. Her tone was one of frustration, not anger. It was a few minutes before I said anything else. Why not go for broke?

"You're packing heat. You could *take care of* Milton. Being a recluse, it could be years before anyone noticed."

Dora let out a short laugh. "It's not that easy, not by a long shot. Besides, maybe as my protégé, you'll *take care of* him."

I raised my eyebrows. She smiled in response.

Neither of us said another word until we reached the mall. We sat down on one of the comfy sofas scattered throughout the mall.

"Okay, how do we play this mysterious game?" I asked.

"We take turns picking people at random and telling each other something we believe about them."

"That's it? That's your game?"

"Let's just try it."

I shrugged and said, "How do you win?"

"It's not a game of winners and losers; it's a game of fun. I'll go first."

After a minute or so, a woman exited Victoria's Secret with a large bag. The woman—probably mid-twenties, blonde hair, six feet tall, and well proportioned—wore a short red silk dress and red heels. Some cleavage was showing.

"What do you think?" Dora asked.

"It's not my turn."

"I say trophy wife."

"Wife? Why not a girlfriend?"

"She's wearing a ring."

"Maybe she wants to keep men away. Besides, that doesn't necessarily mean anything. You're not wearing one."

"Point taken. But I still say trophy wife."

Less than thirty seconds later, a gray-haired man who looked to be in his fifties called to the woman and then approached her. They kissed.

"I win that one," Dora said.

"I thought you said there were no winners or losers."

"Oh! You're right."

I looked around, trying to determine my target. My gaze fell on a distinguished older gentleman heading in our direction. He stopped to look into the Pielino Leather store. When Dora noticed him, she grabbed my arm and stood, pulling me with her.

"Turn around," she said. "Come on."

Dora and I hurried toward the exit. Her breathing was fast and heavy, and she gripped my arm so tight it felt as if it were in a vise. I started to glance back.

"Don't look back," Dora said.

I didn't. Dora let go only after we reached the Lexus. We hopped in and drove off. It was a few minutes before her breathing returned to normal.

"What was that all about?" I asked.

"That man is a superior court judge I've had dealings with."

"You didn't want him to see you?"

"Not exactly. I didn't want him to see *you*."

Me? Why would that matter? Maybe she meant she didn't want the judge to see me *with her*. Would I be in front of the judge one day in something involving her?

When we arrived at my house, Dora walked me to the door.

"Nate, I've dragged this out too long. I was having fun, more fun than I expected. But we need to wrap this up. I'll be back tomorrow morning at eight. You can tell me your decision then."

She gave me a long hug, and I watched her drive off, not moving until the car was out of sight. I felt mournful, as if something—something fun, albeit strange—was ending. I knew what my answer would be. That evening I replayed my time with Dora over and over, enjoying the reminiscing and listening to music, Brahms's Fourth Symphony and Raff's Fourth Symphony. Despite being sad, I also was relieved that this would be over. I avoided thinking about what I might have to do for her.

The next morning, precisely at eight, Dora's Lexus pulled into the driveway. A sense of foreboding flooded over me. Suddenly I was frightened. I'd been backed into a corner. I was going to have to do something terrible, something abhorrent. Dora had aroused a variety of emotions in me during the past few weeks, but none of them dread.

Dora came to the front door carrying a briefcase. I invited

her in. She was beautiful, as usual, but she wore a determined look. She put her briefcase on the kitchen table, opened it, and took a seat. I sat opposite her.

"Sorry, Nate, but I want to get this done."

"Okay." I figured the less I said the better.

"What have you decided?"

"I pass."

"I knew you would. We're at the last option, or I should say requirement—the thing you must do. It's the best option for me. But for you, well . . . you may think this is the worst option. I pray you'll do it. If you don't, I'll see to it that you go to prison for a long, long time."

Dora pulled out an eight-by-ten picture frame. She slid it toward me, face down. I felt a chill run through my body. A tear was running down Dora's face. I was thinking of Milton, the gunrunner, the cruel husband. Maybe he did deserve to die because of all the misery he'd fostered. Could I do it? She turned the picture frame over.

I saw . . .

"You have to—you must—*take care of* this person. With all my money, all my wits, I haven't been able to. I've spent years planning this, Nate, years. You have no idea. You have to help me."

"But—"

"Yes, it's Arly. You have to adopt her. I can't, even though she's my biological daughter. That morning in the park was an audition after a fashion. Arly likes you, and . . . I do too—very much. In a year I will ask you to marry me. You can say yes or you can say no. Either way, you *will be* Arly's father for the rest of your life. Milton doesn't exist; never has. He's fabricated. Here are the adoption papers. Sign, and then I'll answer *all* your questions."

It was silly I know, but I said, "I didn't know Ella Raines's eyes were green."

Dora got up, walked over to me, leaned down, and kissed me on the lips. "Yes, they were," she said as a tear dropped on my cheek.

"Where do I sign?"

The End

2

Completely and Utterly Devoid of Usefulness and Meaning

"If one wanted to crush and destroy a man entirely, to mete out to him the most terrible punishment, all one would have to do would be to make him do work that was completely and utterly devoid of usefulness and meaning," said Fyodor Dostoevsky, a man who came within seconds of being shot by a firing squad. His pardon from the Czar arrived moments before the command—Fire. The man next to Dostoevsky, pardoned too, fell to the ground—insane.

I started my new job with the federal government, the Department of Agriculture, right out of college. When I arrived for work, I was told to go meet my boss, Mr. Sanders, and then go to conference room B for the new-employee orientation at nine. When I arrived at Mr. Sanders's office, his administrative assistant, Persis, ushered me in, and we both took a seat. Mr. Sanders was seated at his desk with his chair turned toward the window. Around his office wall at eye level were large calendars, one for each month. Every single box for each day was written in, but I couldn't tell what was written. As I sat down, Mr. Sanders swiveled his chair around and looked at me. He appeared a bit disheveled. I pretended not to notice.

"Welcome, Mr. Johnson. I—"

"Atwater, sir," Persis chimed in.

"Yes, yes, Mr. Atwater. You'll find I run a tight jet. Our work is vital to the health of the American people—vital. Our division saves thousands of lives each year. You do your job . . ."

I waited for him to finish.

"And Mr. Atwater, don't forget to bring your immunization record in before—"

"That's no longer required, sir," Persis said.

"Since when?"

"The year Nixon died."

"Oh, yes. That's right."

Persis stood, looked at me, and nodded toward the door. I rose and followed her out of the office. Persis went to her desk and sat down.

"You're not old enough to have been here when Nixon died," I said, thinking she looked to be in her late twenties.

"If you want to get ahead, you learn quickly, and we have our own way of dating things. You should come in early or stay late and start memorizing the calendars on Mr. Sanders's walls."

Persis was a brunette, and her hair fell just past her shoulders. Her eyes were light brown with a golden tint. Her lips were coated bright red, and she was wearing a black Dior dress. I know Dior because that's what my mother wore, but only because she worked at the Dior boutique and got a 90 percent discount on customer returns.

"That print behind your desk—a small boat with an oars-
man, white-clad figure, and coffin being rowed toward a small
islet with cypress trees—it doesn't look like a picture that
would be in a government office."

"It's not. I bought it. I put it there to remind me of the futil-
ity of this job, that I'd be here until I die, and to keep people
from bothering me."

"Isle of the Dead? Good choice."

For the first time, she gave me a second look and a smile.

"What makes you think you'll be here until you die?"

"The fringe benefits are too good. I'd be foolish to leave."

"I didn't realize the benefits were that good."

"Yours aren't; mine are."

"Why aren't—"

"You've got five minutes to get to conference room B, Mr.
Atwater. I suggest you be on your way."

"Okay, I'm going."

When I entered the conference room, four other people
with name tags were already seated at a long table. Shell was
reading a dictionary that was on the table; Mike was picking food out of his teeth; Jesse was reading his pocket-sized
Gideon New Testament, and Melva was reading *Philosophiae
Naturalis Principia Mathematica* by Sir Isaac Newton. Maybe
Melva was another Sophie Germain—math whiz. I felt queasy
about taking the job, but with a degree in English and with
most magazines and newspapers not using editors anymore—
which you could tell by the poorly written headlines and articles—my choices were slim.

By ten thirty no one had shown up to give us our orientation. Jesse and Melva were still reading, and Mike was talking about some kind of dental work he needed and how he
would have created Spider-Man first if he'd been born in 1922

like Stan Lee. Shell was on her phone, looking at one of her nine dictionary apps. I thought I'd go find someone to help us, when Jesse put his Bible down, looked at me, and asked, "Have you been saved?"

What direction did I want to go here? I thought about quoting the last few lines of "Thanatopsis," arguably the best poem written by an American but undoubtedly not to Jesse's tastes, which I assumed were not deist. Instead I answered Jesse's question with a story—a story that mixed both truth and fiction.

"Jesse, I—my family and I—have been blessed by the Holy Ghost. My great-great-grandfather was an illiterate man. He was fighting in the Civil War when, three nights straight, he dreamed he was reading the Bible. He heard the words 'If you spread my word, generation after generation of your seed will abide with me in heaven.' On the fourth day he borrowed another man's Bible, and he read it, so he became a preacher, and our family became blessed."

"Ah, but that just sounds like a family legend," Mike said.

Persis had just walked into the room and was putting some copy paper in one of the cabinets.

"Nope, I've seen old newspaper articles about it—more than one—including interviews with some of the men in his regiment," I replied.

"Well, personally, I plan on becoming a Zoroastrian, because one of its tenets is to make money," Mike replied.

At that, Persis stopped as she was about to leave. She turned and looked at Mike.

Melva put down her book.

"You can't be a Zoroastrian," Melva said.

"Why not?" asked Mike.

"You have to be born of Zoroastrian parents. They don't

take converts," Melva replied, before picking up her book to continue reading.

"I'll follow Ayn Rand then," Mike responded.

Persis turned and left the room.

Okay, so a couple of the new employees were fanatics, one about God and one about money. In my experience those things usually meant they were fanatics about other things too.

Jesse, who hadn't uttered a word since his initial question to me, came over and held out his hand to shake. "You're good people," he said.

I shook his hand and debated whether to explain the difference between singular and plural and how sometimes the subjunctive mood could confuse the matter but decided to let it go.

I left to find out the holdup with the orientation. I was told to go back to the conference room; someone would be there shortly. At eleven thirty, someone did show up. We were told that the orientation material—personnel manuals, badges, keys, and other things—weren't ready, and we should go home.

"Do I need to tell my boss I'm leaving?" I asked the HR associate.

"Who's your boss?"

"Mr. Sanders."

"He won't know." That didn't answer my question, but he continued talking as if he'd read my mind. "No, just leave. And tomorrow you and Jesse will get blue badges, while Mike, Shell, and Melva will get red badges. Be sure you get the correct badge."

"Why different-colored badges?"

"Different divisions—the Department of Agriculture has

two divisions that work in this building, and we run a tight jet here."

What the heck is it with the jet? A ship's not good enough?

The next day I decided to stop in and see Persis before going to orientation. When I walked into her office, she wasn't there. I decided to linger. On her six-shelf bookcase was quite an assortment of books: *The Prodigal Women* by Nancy Hale, published in 1942; *The Awakening* by Kate Chopin, copyrighted in 1899; *The Righteous Mind* by Jonathan Haidt; *Just Listen* by Mark Goulston; *In Defence of Rhetoric* by Brian Vickers; *The Art of Seduction* by Robert Greene; *The Rules of Civility* by Amor Towles; *The Six Secrets of Intelligence* by Craig Adams; *The Word Is Murder* by Anthony Horowitz, and many more.

Persis walked into the office. She was wearing another black Dior dress. This time she wore her hair in a bun, and she was wearing black lipstick.

"Oh, hello," she said.

"You look . . . nice," I said. She looked at me with a slight frown, eyes narrowed slightly. "Are all these books yours?"

"Yes."

"How about lunch today in the cafeteria? I'm curious about your books."

"You want to discuss my books?"

"Yes, I've read a few of these. I'd like your opinion on some of them."

"That would be great, except not today. I'll skip supper tonight and wear my redlip . . . we can have lunch tomorrow."

"Okay," I said, wondering what supper and red had to do with it.

Mr. Sanders came in and said, "Persis, when are those reports on the number of lives saved each year due?"

"Warren Harding's birthday, sir."

"Thanks, Persis," he said. Then he left.

Ah, the different way of dating things.

"I'm off to orientation again, Persis."

At orientation we were told there would be two orientations: one for all five of us and one for employees by division. The first thing we were given was the personnel manual. I thought I'd need a hand truck to get it to my office. The HR manager, acknowledging that the manual was a bit much, also gave us a two-thousand-page summary of the manual. Finally, our badges were handed out—mine green.

"Excuse me, I was told I would get a blue badge," I said.

"The colors have been changed to green and yellow. You and Jesse get green badges, and Mike and Melva get yellow badges."

"Why?"

"Why what, Mr. Atwater?"

"Why were the colors changed?"

"Cost savings."

"Cost savings? How does changing the color—"

"Mr. Atwater, are you going to be a troublemaker from day one?"

Actually, it was day two, but I thought it best to let sleeping words lie. "Uh, no."

"And, Shell, here is your purple badge. It seems we can't give you a yellow or a green badge, as it would create an imbalance between the two divisions. Currently only the two division heads have purple badges. You will have the advantage, however, of being able to use either copier."

Either copier?

Officials couldn't decide which division orientation Shell should attend, so they had her wait in the hall.

This job was looking better and better.

Over the next few weeks, I continued to get used to the job. I didn't love it; I didn't hate it. And to my surprise, I was enjoying—for the most part—the company of Persis, Jesse, Mike, Shell, and Melva. Maybe it's natural that we gravitated toward each other because we were hired at the same time—except for Persis.

Persis and I starting eating lunch together two or three times a week. I asked her out on a real date, but she said we should take it slow. Persis had suggested that we eat later in the day. I was excited she wanted to spend time with me alone, but it turned out she preferred that time, if possible, because of her intermittent fasting schedule.

I have read that the happiest people in the world are those with no expectations, because they can't be disappointed. I don't think that's right though. Neuroscience has shown that people often get more satisfaction from anticipation than the act itself. I think it's better if you just remember that what you think you know might be wrong.

My lunches with Persis were the most pleasant part of my days. She didn't wear black lipstick, but red, and she didn't wear black dresses on the days we had lunch, but she always wore Dior. We had interesting conversations.

"Hi, Persis."

"Hello, Atwater."

Since we often ate around three in the afternoon, the cafeteria was mostly empty.

"Have you finished the book I picked out for you last week from my bookshelf?" Persis asked.

"You've got to be kidding. It's a long book, even longer with all that additional text in the margins. I had thought—hoped perhaps—that you were being suggestive by recommending that book."

"And now?"

"Well . . . I think you gave it to me so I could learn from it, to protect myself, so to speak. Even though I'm not far into it, it seems that seduction might be more about getting what you want and less about sex. It's similar to rhetoric, after a fashion."

"That's probably what the ancient Greeks thought too. You might want to read about Peitho, the Greek goddess of persuasion and seduction. I did enjoy *Good Enough,* like you thought I would. I finished it last night. I thought I knew what natural selection and survival of the fittest were. Even Darwin's colleagues chastised him for saying that a species naturally improves year by year, month by month, hour by hour, when there was no proof of this. There is not a mechanism that directs a species to improve; survival is nothing more than chaos—random chance. If anything, you would think that nature would not want a species to change if it was surviving. Darwin's science was biased because of his experience with breeders. Just because farmers were improving their herds by selective breeding, he assumed nature was continuously doing it too. An amazing book. The best book I've read this year. Oh, and I've changed my mind, I *will* go on a picnic with you Saturday."

"Oh, is that because I recommend good books?"

"No, it's because I like you more than I did."

"Like, not love?"

"Atwater, you know my position on love. A mixture of hormones, and—"

"I love it when you call me Atwater."

Persis rolled her eyes and shook her head.

"Persis, I've been meaning to ask you something."

"Go ahead."

"I noticed in orientation when you were putting away the copy paper that you stopped after Mike's comment about becoming Zoroastrian. Why?"

"My parents are Zoroastrian. Haven't you wondered why I can always wear Dior? You know, Zoroastrians and money, like Mike said. I just love generalizations about people."

I knew she despised generalizations.

"Are you Zoroastrian?"

"I'm sure you can tell by now that I'm a freethinker."

"Well, at least now I know why you were named Persis, a name for Persia, where the religion was once Zoroastrianism."

"I guess you're not just another pretty face. I'll tell you what . . . I will go on two picnics with you."

We both laughed.

I saw Mr. Sanders maybe three times a week. Persis always gave me my assignments. Every time I saw Mr. Sanders, he was reading the personnel manual. After a while, my curiosity became too much, and I asked, "Mr. Sanders, why are you always reading the personnel manual?"

He looked up at me. "Mr. Atwater, you have to be ready. You never know when you're going to need an edge."

I nodded as if I knew what he was talking about, turned around, and left his office.

It was at the beginning of my fifth week that the problem started. I went to the copier to make a copy of the latest report from the consulting firm we had on retainer about the dangers of too much cheese consumption. The copier wouldn't work. I checked all the usual suspects but found nothing wrong. Above the copier was a note, "Call Stu at 499 for copier help." I called Stu, and he said he'd be over in a minute or two. I waited until Stu arrived.

"What's wrong with it?" Stu asked.

"I don't know. It's not working."

"Did you examine it?"

Examine it? What the heck? "Yes, all the usual things: checked for paper jams, checked that it had paper, checked the ink level, checked the power cord, checked the capacitor . . ."

He looked at me inquisitively, trying to figure out how I had checked the capacitor, I suppose. He started fumbling around trying to open different parts of the copier.

"Have you done this before?" I asked.

"Sort of."

I didn't respond.

Stu continued, saying, "These two copiers—this one and the one in the other division—are new. They shouldn't be having problems already. The two old copiers, good riddance, are in the basement."

"Maybe I can use one of the old copiers in the basement if you can't get this one working."

"I think not. They're not plugged in, and they take three days to warm up. Besides, we don't have the ink, and some parts are missing. And you have about ten pages there. That'll take about ten minutes to get one copy."

"Three days to warm up, ten minutes to copy ten pages . . . are the machines possessed?"

"You could say that. They're both Xeroxes purchased in 1960 and weigh about two thousand pounds each."

"They have been here since 1960, and you've just replaced them?"

"We're not exactly cutting edge."

"Sheesh, you've got that right."

"This might take a while. I'll call you when it's working."

"Okay," I said, going back to my office and wondering if

maybe I'd need to start taking things home to copy them.

Stu called me about two hours later. Some glue had gotten on one of the rollers, which he replaced, so the copier was working again.

Later our group had lunch together. At some point the HR director came walking by and stopped to ask Persis a question.

"Persis, when is that report due that Mr. Sanders wants?"

"Elizabeth Taylor's wedding anniversary," Persis said.

I burst out laughing, shook my head, and said rather loudly, "Which one?"

The cafeteria went deadly silent, and everyone turned to look at me. I looked down and went back to eating my lunch. *I hadn't memorized all the calendars yet.*

The next day Persis and I had lunch together.

"Persis, can I tell you about my dream from last night?"

"Sure."

"I was building a brick wall about six feet high. I was building it from left to right, and it looked perfect. About ten feet to my left was another person following in my path, tearing down the wall, not with a sledgehammer, but with a chisel. He was undoing my work."

We both know what that's about don't we, our jobs."

"Don't you think that our jobs are completely and utterly devoid of usefulness and meaning—considering?"

"You mean considering what the other division does? But Atwater, at least the jobs are providing employment for people. Isn't that a good thing?"

"Well, yes, but couldn't the money be better spent?"

"Yes, but it could also be spent less wisely."

"But this work hollows out the very soul of a person. It crushes the very nature of a man or woman. It makes your work meaningless, which may be the worst thing."

"It's not natural that things be perfect, is it? Think of what you learned by reading *Good Enough.* Even if no humans were on earth, some species of animals and plants would vanish. Contrary to National Geographic TV shows, nature isn't perfect either. Do you think God is perfect?"

"Well, of course, it's the nature of God to be perfect. God wouldn't be God if not perfect."

Persis smiled at me, but not with her mouth, with her eyes, something that's hard to do. It's something that has to be learned, be practiced, as it's not a natural expression, so I've heard.

"Atwater, it's in people's nature to believe that some things are perfect—God, nature, ants. It's our assumptions that limit us."

"Ants?"

"Yes, ants. Remember those movies you watched in high school science class? They showed colonies of thousands of ants all working together, every ant doing its job. But now they have discovered that some ants are not working wholeheartedly. Some are even slackers, in a manner of speaking. I do think the more intelligent a person is, the more important it is that the work be meaningful. I feel exactly the way you do about the job. Isle of the Dead, remember? I enjoy hearing about your dreams."

"I'm glad."

Early the next day, I needed to make some copies. The copier wasn't working again, and I called Stu.

When Stu arrived, he started his examination. "I'll call you when it's working."

"Okay, but I'm going over to the other division to use their copier."

Stu chuckled slightly. "Good luck with that."

I was sure I could finagle it and walked down the hall to the other division.

"You're forbidden to use this copier," the division secretary told me.

"Why?" I asked.

"You're wearing a green employee badge."

"So?" I asked with squinted eyes, tilted head, and an inquisitive smile.

She pointed to a sign over *their* copier that read, "For Use by Yellow-Badge Employees Only." "Red" had been crossed out and "Yellow" written in with crayon.

"Because I work in the other division, I can't use your copier?"

"That's right."

"But why?"

She pulled out the unabridged personnel manual.

Oh, no! Not the unabridged personnel manual!

"See," she said, "Section 4.3b(8): Any device that replicates information that is used to create synergy between named organizations can only be used by organization subordinates within the same department's division unless the organization's facilities require the use of substantially the same trajectory by organization subordinates to achieve their functional location, notwithstanding anything else in the manual, unless referred to exclusively, or not exclusively, if amended prior to the date of the original accord."

"So, I can only use your copier if I have a yellow badge?"

"Or purple."

Purple, ah . . . there's Shell's advantage. And Shell became very popular for the next day or so until two things happened. First, the HR director went over Shell's badge with a green marker, turning it gray. Second, the copier in the other division started breaking, too. Both copiers broke continuously. Work came to a standstill, and Mr. Sanders started staying home, and it didn't count as vacation time. It had something to do with inadequately functioning tools for more than half the workday, as referenced somewhere in the unabridged personnel manual. The edge Mr. Sanders was talking about, I guess. Most people kept coming to work but often would spend the day online or reading books. Occasionally an employee showed up in Persis's office asking to borrow a book, which interfered with my flirting, or hers, depending on your perspective.

The next time Persis and I had lunch together, just us, I decided to ask her a question I had tried to ask her before. "Persis, on my first day at work, you told me your fringe benefits were better than mine."

"Did I?"

"Yes."

"And you have been wondering about that . . . about . . . me?"

"Well, yes."

"I'm not sure why I would have said that . . . silly me."

Although Persis and I both had a profound sense of curiosity and a love of reading as a result, she could still be mysterious.

I told my mother about Persis and our conversation about her fringe benefits. My mother chuckled and said, "Dear, dear, boy, I hope you like her too. Maybe she's another Anna."

My mother and I smiled at each other knowingly. I wondered.

One day during lunch, when neither Jesse nor Mike happened to be there, Melva, Shell, Persis and I had a conversation that was the beginning of the end.

"I found out that for the past three weeks a private

investigator has been looking into why the copiers are constantly breaking," Persis said, "and tomorrow there will be a company-wide meeting so the investigator can explain it."

"They should have just asked me," Melva said. Melva thought of herself as a female Sherlock Holmes. As sagacious as she was, she certainly could have been.

"They should have asked you?" Shell inquired.

"Yes, the copiers are being sabotaged. I just don't know why," Melva responded.

"Sabotaged? Who is sabotaging them?" Persis asked.

"It was easy to figure out. Just check the log. It was always one of two people who had either used the copier just before it broke or reported it broken before they could use it. It was always either Jesse or Mike," Melva said.

That made sense. And I knew why they were doing it—fanatics.

The next day all employees gathered in the auditorium. The investigator reported that the copiers had been sabotaged. Hidden cameras had identified the culprits. No one said a thing while the investigator played the surveillance tapes.

The tapes showed Jesse, time after time, messing with the other division's copier. Sometimes the stealth operation was quick: open the copier and squirt something behind the rollers. At other times it went on for several minutes, for example when he removed a part and spread the contents of a small envelope, perhaps metal filings, over it before he replaced the part. On the next tape Mike was doing similar things to our copier.

The private investigator explained that the actions of Mike and Jesse, the saboteurs, were rational, were to be expected, and were in accordance with each division's mission. The investigator asked if anyone understood his point. I raised my hand. He asked me to stand and state each division's mission.

Upon standing I said, "My division's mission is to promote the health of the American people by encouraging them to eat less cheese because eating too much cheese is unhealthy. The mission of the other division is to encourage the American public to eat more cheese because eating more cheese helps dairy farmers." I sat down.

Dostoevsky would have already quit. I quit my job at the Department of Agriculture the next day. Persis turned in her notice too, and we left hand in hand. As we walked, swinging our arms together, I knew our finding each other was destiny. My thoughts of Persis mixed with thoughts of another woman of destiny, Anna, whom I never knew, but knew of. Anna had been such a wonderful wife. A wife like no other. She, like other women growing up during the sixties, was educated, talented, able, and her own woman. A woman who would care for her husband, handle his business affairs, have frank discussions with him, and love him as no other woman could have. I hoped that one day Persis would feel about me the way Anna felt about her husband.

"He was the kindest, the gentlest, the wisest, and most generous of all the men I have ever known," said Anna about her husband, Fyodor Dostoevsky, who died in 1881. Anna, and her cadre of trailblazing women during the 1860s, was something special. She had become a philatelist, the first female in Russia to do so, because she wanted to disprove her husband's ideas about the fickleness of women and their inability to stick with something. And she certainly proved it many times over. In 1918, when Anna died, Russia was in the throes of a revolution. It's not known what happened to her stamp collection.

The End

3

Alina, the Tunnel, and the Bank

Since my family had gone to visit relatives, I spent all day digging in the tunnel. After three years, you would think I would have been tired of it, tired of the still air, the dirt, the grime, the sore back, the money for flashlight batteries, the showers, the dirty fingernails. Only seventeen, I'd spent many days after school and on weekends digging alone. I hadn't measured the length of the tunnel in two months, but I knew it extended under the street because of all the noise and vibrations. I estimated that I was fifty feet from the bank's basement wall. If I could get into that bank, my life would change forever. I would be able to do anything and have anything I wanted; I had to get into that bank.

The digging had started three years earlier when John and Karl, both sixteen, and me, fourteen, were playing explorer, something we often did. One day we snuck into the basement of an abandoned building close to my house.

"Karl, this bookcase isn't flat against the wall," John said. "It looks like there's a hole behind it. Help me move it."

No one had been in that basement for years. Dust was layered on empty shelves and dirt was piled in the corners. The translucent glass at the top of the walls was high enough to filter the daylight that beamed inside. Karl and I helped John move the bookcase, which revealed a large hole that had been carved out of the wall. Beyond it was a tunnel high enough to stand in, but it was pitch dark, so we didn't go in, as we had no flashlights.

"Where do you suppose it goes?" John asked.

"To the bank," all three of us said in unison.

The bank was across the street on the other side of the wall—the wall that marked the border between our countries, the wall that butted up against the street on the other side of the road and ran not only the entire length of the street but also the entire length of the city. The bank was in their country, but we knew that the bank was full of American money. People in most other countries preferred to use American dollars.

"John," Karl asked, "what would you do with a million dollars?"

"I'd buy a house in the country, a fancy car, and hire people to cook and clean for me."

"Me too," Karl said, "and I'd go on vacations in the Mediterranean, and I'd want lots of girlfriends."

We all laughed. Karl didn't play football like John did, so he didn't have girls hanging around him.

"Alina, what about you?" Karl asked. "What would you want?"

"Freedom, the freedom to go wherever I wanted and to think whatever I wanted."

"That's Alina, always the dreamer," John said.

That's what my dad called me too—a dreamer—but a dreamer with talent, which is what a dreamer needs, he would say. He told me I had insight into people and a way with words—that I was a talented writer. When I was ten, I wrote a fictional story about a family and their relatives. All the characters were snooty, except the father and the daughter. When I gave the story to my family members to read, some were offended because they saw reflections of themselves. But my father loved the story.

"I'd want things too," I said, "things that our family can't afford to give us because they don't have the money or belong to the privileged class."

We found a key to the building on a peg that had been drilled into the basement wall, so we locked the window that we had opened to climb into the building.

"Okay," Karl said, "we'll rendezvous here after class on Thursday at five—and bring flashlights. And one more thing: on Thursday let's tell each other one thing we would buy with the money. It has to be unusual and special to us."

We all agreed.

On Thursday we all met at the building with our flashlights and our wishes.

"John, you start," I said. "What's your unusual desire?"

"I would buy a peddler's wagon. When I was little and living in the country, a peddler would come by every month. His wagon seemed magical and the peddler a wizard. It had everything you could want—dresses, shirts, pots and pans, toys, medicine for both animals and people, crayons, jewelry, tools, everything. Even today, nothing gives me as much joy as seeing a peddler's wagon coming down the street."

I moved over to John and rubbed his shoulder. "Karl, you're next," I said.

"I would buy a bicycle. Not just any bicycle—the bicycle owned by Jack Steel."

John and I glanced at each other and wondered, *Who is Jack Steel?*

Karl continued, "The bicycle that was given to Jack Steel by Al Capone after Jack's bicycle had been crushed by a milk delivery truck. Al Capone was buying a newspaper from Jack when the truck careened into Jack's unoccupied bicycle right in front of them. Jack started to cry. Capone took him by the hand, went across the street to Sears and Roebuck, and they came out with a brand-new bicycle. I learned about that from a TV show called *The Bad Americans*."

John and I looked at each other again—still wondering.

Karl continued. "When I become a doctor, I'll keep the bicycle in my office as a reminder, a reminder that all people deserve my help as a doctor. I know that's not what's popular or the attitude we're encouraged to take, but it's how I feel."

John walked over to Karl and said, "Karl, I know you feel that way. I think it's because of that man and his wife who were shot and killed while trying to cross the wall, shot by border patrol officers, like Alina's father. The couple fell at your feet—dead. I give you slack because you experienced that trauma at such a young age and because I love you like a brother. But we disagree about the wall. People who try to get over the wall, get to a new life, are breaking the law, and we don't need those kind here. That's why border patrol officers are allowed to shoot them."

John hugged Karl. I hugged them both.

"Now, Alina, it's your turn," John said.

"I want a book, a book that mesmerizes me with words, ideas, dialogue, longing, and longing's adversary—satisfaction. I don't know what book it is yet. But when I find it, I'll buy it. And if I can't find it, I'll write it."

John and Karl looked at each other with raised eyebrows and nodded.

"Okay, guys," I said, "let's get to our tunnel and start digging." I pulled them both toward the basement.

The tunnel was impressive. In most places it was high enough for us to stand; it sloped down about two feet and then leveled off. Various tools were propped up along its dirt wall. We calculated that the tunnel was roughly one-fourth of the way to the bank. With money as the catalyst, both John and Karl wanted to continue with the tunnel. I did too.

After a year of digging, John and Karl's motivation waned, but mine didn't. One day when we were digging, I could tell their hearts weren't in it, so I decided to try an idea while we were resting outside the tunnel entrance.

"Guys, I have a thought. Let's put up a *will have* list on the bulletin board."

"What's that?" John asked.

"On the bulletin board over on that wall, we'll each cut out five pictures from magazines, or whatever, and tack them up—pictures of what we'll buy with the money we get from the bank. We can switch out the pictures when we find something better. Eventually, we'll expand the list to ten things—maybe more."

"I like that," John said. "It's fun thinking about all the things we could buy."

"Karl, what do you think?" I asked.

"It can't hurt."

It worked like a magic elixir. We progressed like we did in the initial days. A few months later, I again spiced things up. I tacked up a picture of an attractive model on each of their lists, and I changed the picture each month. Our productivity continued to soar. And Mom thought I didn't know the first thing about boys.

We dug after school and almost always on weekends. We were making great progress and had reached the street. But when Karl and John graduated from high school, they stopped digging. Karl moved away to go to college, and John joined the border patrol and was assigned to a different city. I never saw either of them again. On my own, I figured it would take another year to complete the tunnel. My motivation to reach the bank never wavered, so I kept digging.

My mother worked at a sewing plant on the other side of town. She would catch the bus early and arrive home late, but not too late to fix supper. She liked to cook. I loved my mother, but she prattled incessantly. If you contradicted what she said, she seemed to be deaf to your comments. She was constantly after me to date one of the boys who went to one of the first-rate schools. The schools where high-ranking government officials and other people of importance could send their children.

"Marry someone whose father has a government job," my mother advised. "It always seems their children get the best jobs. Then you wouldn't have to work at a sewing plant."

It was vexing. Besides, I knew I'd never work at the sewing plant. Especially if I could make it to the bank.

My father worked at night, which was great. He would see me off to school in the morning and be home when I returned. He did most of the housework and never complained about washing my clothes, which were always filthy. For many years my father had patrolled the wall at night. He was the best-known border patrol officer on the force and had a stellar reputation. I knew he used to be the best marksman of all the border patrol officers. He had the highest kill and capture rate too. I didn't like to think about that. He was John's hero and the reason why he became a Federal Border Patrol officer. Eventually my father was transferred to a desk job, but he still worked nights.

Despite my father's job, I not only loved him, I adored him. He was my hero and always encouraged me. He was never short with me, and he never belittled any of my thoughts or questions. He never pushed me to do one thing or another. Although it seems odd, I never thought he'd be angry with me for tunneling to the bank, but I never dared tell him, just in case.

My tunnel was still under the road, but I had calculated it to be fifteen feet from the bank's basement. I wouldn't have to worry about getting through the border wall itself because it stopped about two feet under the ground, and I would be completely below it. But one day when I got home from school something unexpected happened.

"Alina," my father said, "I've left something on your bed."

"Okay," I replied, and I hurried upstairs to put my books away and change, after which I glanced at my bed. The item that my father had mentioned looked like a poster. It was about three feet long and rolled up with a rubber band. After unrolling it, I studied it for about twenty seconds before I realized what it was. In shock, I dropped it on the floor and fell back onto my bed. I was overcome with fright and confusion, feeling more scared than I'd ever been. I could feel my heart pounding. My mind would have been racing, but it didn't know where to start. There was a knock on the door, and my father stepped into the room.

"I thought I'd bring you a glass of water, dear." He quietly moved to the dresser, stepping over the paper on the floor, and placed the glass there. He turned and calmly headed to the door to leave. "Oh," he said, pointing to the paper on the floor,

"I wouldn't leave that lying around. Perhaps put it in your hiding place in the basement. You know, where you keep those politically incorrect documents and books—*Huckleberry Finn, The Second Sex,* the copy of the Declaration of Independence. Even Woodrow Wilson said Americans should not read parts of the Declaration of Independence, because it's subversive. Let's see how does it start? Oh, yes, *'When, in the course of human events, it becomes necessary for one people to dissolve the political bands which have connected them with another, and to assume, among the powers of the earth, the separate and equal station to which the laws of nature and of nature's God entitle them.'* And then it ends, *'with a firm reliance on the protection of Divine Providence, we mutually pledge to each other our lives, our fortunes, and our sacred honor.'* One more thing, Alina. I think you'll find the conversation at supper this evening helpful."

With that, my father left. What had just happened? I was at a loss. I wasn't quite as scared after my father said all that, but I was utterly confused.

After about fifteen minutes, I felt calm enough to pick up the poster from the floor. It looked like an architect's drawing with lines, measurements, brief notes, and descriptions inscribed all over it. It was a document from the city planning department, a drawing of what was below the street—the street my tunnel was under. It showed the locations of water pipes, electrical power cables, and sewer lines. As I studied it more closely, I realized that a water pipe was close to my tunnel, but it didn't seem to be a cause for concern, because the pipe was in the middle of the street, and I had already passed that point.

My father knew. He knew about the tunnel, and he must have realized it was leading to the bank and under the wall, the wall that was his job to secure, the wall that no one was allowed to cross over or tunnel under.

My thoughts were muddled as I stumbled downstairs to supper. I hung on every word said during supper, and then, finally, the moment arrived.

"Dear," my father said while glancing at my mother, "there will be a little more traffic on our street next week."

"Is that right? What's going on?"

"Earlier this week I talked to some city workers one block over, across from that abandoned building near the wall. It turns out there's a leak in the water pipe under the street. Next week the city will be digging to fix the pipe. The street will be blocked for about a week."

I dropped my fork, and I knew I went pale. I felt lightheaded but otherwise managed to remain composed.

"I hope they don't make a mess of it," my mother said. "You know those city workers. Lazy pigs, they're always taking two-hour lunches, taking an hour to do something that could be done in five minutes. I bet they'll take three weeks to finish the street. You would think that—."

"It shouldn't be a big mess, dear. They know exactly where the leak is and will only have to dig a small hole no more than two feet across and no more than a few inches below the pipe."

"Why, I saw one of those city workers throw a candy wrapper on the sidewalk just the other day. Mrs. Anderson's dog ate it, and she had to take him to the vet. And the vet bill was—"

"I tell you what, dear. I'll check on those city workers during the day. I'll keep tabs on their progress." Dad looked at me and winked.

"Good idea. Mrs. Grayson's son works for the city, and, well, we all know what kind of . . ." My mother's voice trailed off.

I could see her mouth moving, but I wasn't hearing anything. I figured my brain was using its energy to try to make sense of all this information.

That night after I had gotten into bed and before my dad headed to work, he knocked on my door to wish me goodnight, which he always did.

"Come in."

"Goodnight, dear Alina."

"Goodnight, Dad. Dad?"

"Yes."

"How much do you know about what I'm doing?"

"I know exactly what you're doing, Alina, and I know why you're doing it. I've known for years about you, John, Karl, and the tunnel. I knew you'd keep digging after they left. This is exactly what I expected."

"But how?"

"Alina, it's best if we talk of this no more, at least for now. You'll understand later. Don't try to figure it out. Just know that nothing that you learned today should change what you're doing, although I wouldn't work while the pipe is being repaired."

"Thank you, Dad."

"Goodnight, Alina. I'll see you tomorrow."

I didn't think it was possible to love my dad any more than I already did, but I was wrong.

Once the city workers started repairing the pipe, Dad gave a full account of their progress at supper every night. By Friday the workers were finished, and my tunnel remained undiscovered.

Several months later, I finally reached the bank's basement wall. I told Dad before Mom came home.

"When are you planning to break through?"

"I'll start Saturday after the bank closes."

"Good. What will the code be?"

"If men were angels, no government would be necessary."

"Ah, James Madison; excellent. I'll be on the lookout. Your mother and I will go to Aunt Sophie's this Saturday and stay the weekend."

"Dad?"

"Yes, Alina?"

"How is it you're helping me? You with the highest kill-and-capture rate for people crossing the wall and your reputation."

"Alina, my darling daughter, you can get a reputation by doing something and doing it well or by not doing it and allowing people to think you did."

"I don't understand."

"Before I became a border patrol officer, I decided that I needed to be the best marksman on the force, so I practiced and practiced. When we had marksmanship tests, I had the best scores. On my first day of work, I scored the highest of any new recruit and better than any officer on the entire force. Something like that gets around. One day I'm patrolling the wall with another officer, and we see someone on the wall, or near it. I could shoot well enough to get close but not hit the person. Well, maybe my fellow officer does hit the person. Everyone, even the other officer I was with, thinks I hit the person because I'm a better shot. I patrolled the wall for fifteen years and never shot anybody."

"Oh, Dad." I hugged him as hard as I could.

"Alina, I can't change the world. I do the best I can under the circumstances and try to keep you and your mother safe. But you—you, my dear, can change the world. You're different. I know you can get into that bank and get what you want, what you need."

"Dad, I love you."

"I love you, too. And you'll be finishing something I started a long time ago."

"What do you mean?"

"Did you, Karl, and John ever wonder who started that tunnel?"

"You?" I said as goosebumps covered my body.

"Yes, dear girl."

That Saturday when I woke up, my parents had already gone to Aunt Sophie's. It was better that way, though I wanted so much to give Dad one last hug.

I finally broke through the basement wall by noon that Sunday. I raced upstairs and peeked out a window to be sure I was in the right place. I was. As I expected, the president of the bank called the police Monday morning, yet there was no story in the newspaper about a bank robbery, a missing girl, or a mysterious tunnel. Several weeks later I placed a personal ad in the paper that read, "*If men were angels, no government would be necessary. Love, Always A.*"

Dad had made me promise to tell my story after he and Mom died. He said I was one of the youngest and probably the only person inspired by the Declaration of Independence to cross the wall. Dad said even he didn't know how many people were killed trying to get over or under the wall that separated our communist East Berlin from *free* West Berlin.

The End

4

The Wrong School Bus

I remember that day in 1966, the first day of third grade, when I got on the wrong school bus to go home. I was on the wrong bus because I had followed her, not thinking about anything but her. It was her face. Her face was mesmerizing and had captured me body and soul.

That morning my mother had safety-pinned the bus number to my shirt. I had ripped it off before any of the other kids saw it. A third grader doesn't need childish reminders. Besides, I had memorized the number. When I followed her onto the bus, I wasn't thinking about buses or numbers or even where I was.

I sat next to her and looked at her now and then. I couldn't look for long, as I'd start feeling warm all over. I had been sitting next to her for a while when I looked out the window. The scenery was unfamiliar to me, and I was jolted back to reality. I knew right away that I was on the wrong bus.

I wasn't worried; I didn't give it a second thought. After all, I'd had issues with school buses last year in Paris. My father was in the diplomatic corps, and we lived on the French economy—that is, not in diplomatic housing where most other

American diplomats lived. I went to a school for diplomats' children and often got on the wrong bus. Or I got on the right bus but with a bus driver who couldn't figure out where to drop me off. Occasionally my father tracked down the bus to get me. I always got home safely. Since we were back in the States, How much of a problem could it be?

"Hello," I said to her.

"Hi," she replied. I had never felt so warm.

"It's a pretty day."

"Yes, it is."

"My name is Joey. I'm in Ms. Rizzo's class."

"Me too." She tilted her head and smiled at me. "My name is Susan."

I'd never felt so wonderful. I thought I must be in heaven. Her eyes seemed to reach into me and tickle my heart. I wanted to be around her, to look at her face forever.

"Susan, I got on the wrong bus."

"Oh, no." Even though her face had a concerned expression, it still seemed like the face of an angel.

"Can I get off with you, and maybe your mother can call my mom to come pick me up?"

"Sure, my stop is next."

As things were, it seemed like the easiest way for me to get home.

After we got off the bus and started walking to Susan's house, she said, "Maybe we can play until your mom comes to get you."

"Okay." I didn't even flinch at the possibility that we might play with dolls. At that moment Susan was my world.

I walked into the house with Susan and followed her back into the kitchen where a woman was standing over the sink.

As the woman turned around, she said, "Well, how was . . .

oh, and who do we have here?"

"This is Joey, Mom. He got on the wrong school bus."

"Hello, Joey. I am Susan's mom, Mrs. Smith."

"Hi."

"Well, let's get you some snacks. Then we'll see if we can get in touch with your mother," Mrs. Smith said.

After milk and cookies and some conversation about the first day of class, Mrs. Smith called my mom. I should say, she tried to. No one picked up the phone, and I didn't know my dad's work number.

Meanwhile, Susan had asked me if I wanted to play chess.

"Chess!" I exclaimed excitedly.

"Yes, you seem surprised."

"I don't know any girls who play chess."

"Mom says it has been a man's world and women should compete like Helen Keller, Amelia Earhart, Sofia Kovalevskaya, and Virginia Hall."

I had no idea who those people were. "Uh huh," I said as we started playing chess.

Lately, I often think about the times Joey used to come over and play with my daughter, Susan. Susan and Joey's playing together seems to me now—forty years later—almost a magical time. Joey's hair was light brown; he had a sweet face and was polite. In those days we weren't afraid for our children as parents are today. I wondered if Joey was afraid. He didn't seem to be. I was surprised Joey beat Susan in chess. Susan was rarely beaten by children her age or by children a few years older. I think she was glad she lost. I was happy to see her gracious reaction. I had taught her to

relish losing because it was the best way to learn and get bet-
ter. While watching them play, I noticed Joey would often
gaze at Susan's face with the most sedate, loving look. Even
today, Joey's expression remains the most explicit reflection
of love I've ever seen. Now that I'm older, sixty-eight, I find
myself often thinking about love, which surprises me. I'm cu-
rious about it, but I don't want to read about it; I'm afraid to.
Afraid it will spoil what I know, or what I think I know about
love, and I don't want that.

After thirty minutes of trying to reach my mom on the
phone, Mrs. Smith decided she would drive me home.

"Joey, what is your address?"

"Two-fourteen Greenwell Drive."

"Greenwell Drive? I don't know where that is, but I'll find
out."

After I made each chess move, I would watch Susan's face
as she studied the board. I wasn't thinking about anything
else during those moments but her. God couldn't have made a
more beautiful face. I was happy, so happy.

Mrs. Smith came into the den where Susan and I were
playing chess. She found out where Greenwell Drive was and
suggested we head over, since my mom might be worried.

I kept a city map in the car and found Greenwell Drive.
When Susan, Joey, and I pulled up to Joey's house that day,
a group of women was gathered in the front yard. They were
about to start canvassing the neighborhood looking for Joey.

Naturally Joey's mom and the neighborhood women were relieved to see Joey safe and sound. As the women returned to their homes, Joey's mom invited Susan and me inside. Before I knew it, an hour had passed. We enjoyed each other's company so much that we decided Joey should take the bus home with Susan once a month, and then I'd drive him home, assuming, of course, that Susan and Joey had no objections, which they didn't.

I thought Joey's mom and I would become good friends, but that didn't happen. As with all young mothers, our time went to everyone else. We rarely had time to relax together during drop-offs. Joey's family moved out of state at the end of the school year. In spite of the fact that we promised to keep in touch, we didn't.

When Mrs. Smith and Susan took me home that day, I was disappointed when they had to leave. The days I went home with Susan were the happiest of my childhood. Susan and I would play chess, but we did a lot of other things too: built paper airplanes to see whose could go the farthest, played kickball, pretended to be explorers tromping through the woods, rode bicycles—I rode her brother's—and played other silly games we made up. I had a couple of favorites, teacher-student was one. We pretended to be in class with Susan as the teacher and me as the student. She would wear a pair of glasses without lenses, and I would read from a book she picked out, poetry usually. I didn't understand most of it, but she seemed to. Sometimes she would just stare at me as I read. It was the most wonderful sensation. If I mispronounced a word, the teacher would have me get the dictionary and correct my pronunciation.

One day—I don't know why—I asked Susan, "Susan, will you marry me?" The second after I said the words, I felt embarrassed.

"I'm too young," Susan said. "Besides, Mom says I need to finish college, have a career, and sow any wild oats before marriage."

What the heck. I didn't know what any of that meant. I was embarrassed and wanted to drop the subject anyway.

Over time, does love change? Does love turn into some-thing else? I can't think of love without thinking about Joey. My girlfriends and I get into conversations about love, long-ing, passion, and marriage. We try to remember what love felt like when we were young, and we can't. Some of us are sad about that. Others are glad, glad we're older, glad we've left behind the emotional turbulence of young love. When I think of pure love, I think of the look on Joey's face when he looked at Susan. He was too young for his love to be any-thing but that, pure. And when we girls talk about what love means to us now, now that we're older, I think of that scene in the movie Fifth Avenue Girl *when Ginger Rogers's char-acter, a young woman, asks Walter Connelly, an older man who's been married for many years, "You're still in love with your wife aren't you?" And he says, "Well, no, but you see, after a certain amount of time, when love goes away, some-thing else is left in its place which is even more important."*

The End

5

Not Once but Three Times

Bill ate dinner every Friday at Fred's Diner. A weekly treat that he allowed himself as a fifty-two-year-old bachelor. A bachelor because he had never found *the one*. Sometimes that happens to a man in spite of being *a catch*. And he was a gentleman who didn't deserve what befell him that day.

Before Bill sat down, he'd always spend a few minutes pleasantly chatting with Fred, and that day was no exception.

"Hi, Bill. I've been waiting all week to tell you; I went to see the movie *Richard Jewell*. I remember when all that happened, but wow! And now he's gone, but at least his mother is alive to see the public vindication."

"I don't know how much satisfaction it gives her now," Bill said glumly.

"Why does that happen, people jumping to conclusions?"

"We could discuss that all night. Besides, most people, most of the time, are guided by emotion, not reason. Look at Sir Arthur Conan Doyle. You'd figure the person who wrote Sherlock Holmes—who was the epitome of using reasoning— would be a man of reason himself. Yet, he believed in fairies," Bill said, while picturing Sherlock Holmes saying "Give me the facts" before he could solve a crime.

While eating, Bill would read the newspaper and think for a bit while his food settled. Fred didn't mind Bill just sitting there reading and thinking; the diner was seldom full.

The woman, her name was Lily, was in Bill's sightline but at the opposite end of the diner. Bill's eyes wandered between his food, the paper, and Lily. Perhaps he was distracted by Lily, something that could easily happen, considering.

If I were working the front desk at the local police station, I'd say Lily was in her early forties, five-seven, 125 pounds, jet-black hair framing her bright-white face, and blue eyes. She had a PhD in chemistry. That day she wore a button-up sleeveless white blouse with ruffles, a short white pleated skirt, and white high-heel sandals.

But as one person noticing another, I was taken aback by her face, which radiated adroitness. The kind of face one rarely sees during a lifetime. She reminded me of the actress Heddy Lamar, who was supposed to be the most beautiful woman in Hollywood in the 1930s and 1940s, and who in 1942 received a patent—along with her friend the composer George Antheil—for a frequency spread communication system designed to prevent homing torpedoes from being jammed. An important breakthrough, considering World War II was in progress at the time.

A few minutes after Lily finished her meal, she stood up and walked over to Bill's table. Anyone watching would have noticed her walk of determination.

"Excuse me, I understand you're Bill Smith," Lily said.

"Yes, I am," replied Bill, gazing up at Lily.

Lily looked at Bill, raised her purse to her chest, unsnapped the clasp, removed her pistol, pointed it at Bill's chest, and pulled the trigger. Not once but three times.

Fred and a nearby customer knocked over a table scrambling to subdue Lily. They forced her into a chair, took the pistol, and stood over her until the police arrived.

Bill didn't look good; it was too late to help him.

When the police arrived, a crowd had gathered outside Fred's. The officers went into Fred's and then over to Lily and took charge of her pistol and purse. One of the officers took out his notepad and read Lily her rights—which she waived—and started taking her statement.

"After I placed my order, Bill Smith started leering at me. This continued all evening," Lily said calmly, unconcerned.

"It's not a crime for someone to look at you," the officer said to Lily.

"He wasn't looking; he was leering, which suggests a lascivious interest or malicious intent. I could virtually see his pupils dilating. I wanted to put a stop to it."

"Was he wearing glasses?" asked the officer.

"No," said Lily.

"How did you know his name?" the officer said.

"I asked that man over there," Lily said, pointing to Fred.

"Well, you can't be too careful these days. So, how often has this been happening?" the officer asked.

"How often?" Lily inquired.

"Yes, Mr. Smith leering at you. Was it every day, several times a week, once a month?" the officer said.

"Tonight was the first time," Lily replied.

"What? This is the first time it's happened, and you pulled a pistol on the guy?"

"Yes," Lily said with a tone of righteous confidence.

"That's cold," the officer said bluntly.

The officer got up and walked over to Fred and several of the patrons to ask them some questions. Then he walked back to Lily and sat down.

"Miss," the officer said, "Bill Smith is nearsighted."

"What?" said Lily.

The officer repeated, "He is nearsighted. When he eats, he takes his glasses off so he can see his food and read his paper. He doesn't put his glasses back on until he gets up to leave. He couldn't have been leering at you. He can't see that far."

"Oh, my God! What have I done?" Lily said in a wavering voice. "What do I do now?"

"Well, my suggestion," said the officer, "is apologize to Bill for ruining his shirt with the permanent ink, offer to pay for a new one, and tell him you'll lose the water pistol."

The End

6

How I Met My Second Wife

Lisa and I had been married for about a year before we agreed to a divorce. When you're dating, you're on your best behavior. And if both parties are masquerading, feigning an interest in the other's interests and beliefs in an effort to be polite, it unfortunately takes longer for them to truly know each other.

We had only dated for three months before we got married, and after the marriage, it didn't take long before a gulf grew between us. I realized we should get a divorce before Lisa did. At first she opposed the idea because she thought it was a reflection on her. But after talks with her younger sister, Langley, she also realized it would be the best thing to do.

I met Langley only once before the marriage. But as I spent more time with Lisa's family, I started seeing more of Langley because she would edit stories I wrote in my spare time. There was an easiness being around her with no hint of pretense. She had a maturity about her well beyond her seventeen years. I was more at ease around Langley than around any woman I had ever met. And, well, I couldn't ask Langley out; not while still married to her sister. After the divorce, I would have to wait a modicum of time. But how long? Even then, would it be possible?

I had moved out of the apartment I shared with Lisa six weeks before the divorce. My new complex was replacing the water lines to the laundry facilities, so I headed to the laundromat. I had only a vague idea of how to do the laundry. I figured I could at least get my clothes cleaner than they were and not destroy them in the process. That's where I met Ginger.

When I entered the laundromat, the right side was crowded, but the left side wasn't, so I went left. I started putting my clothes into a washer.

"Excuse me, that's my washer," said the woman who looked to be my age, was my height, brunette, and had jet-black eyelashes and bright red lipstick.

"Oh, I'm sorry. I didn't realize." How was I supposed to know it was her washer as there was no basket or clothes on it?

"You don't do this often, do you?"

"First time."

"Your wife doesn't do it for you?"

"Wife?"

"You *are* wearing a wedding ring."

"Oh, that. We're divorced—or, rather, divorcing."

"Oh," she said as she lifted a pair of pink panties out of my laundry basket. "Your wife's?"

We both burst out laughing.

"Yes," I said, feeling my face warming.

"Hi, I'm Ginger Raines."

"Rocklin, Rocklin Evans. Nice to meet you. So, how would I have known this was your washer?"

"Well, the washers and dryers on this side of the laundromat are reserved. You pay a monthly fee and reserve them online."

"I'd never heard of such a thing. Is it worth the money?"

"For me, yes. I'm in medical school and don't have the time to wait on washers and dryers. You see the people on the other side; they're having to wait."

I started to take my clothes out of the washer.

"Don't do that, Rocklin. I don't have a lot of laundry today—we can share the washer."

As her hand touched mine, I felt a shock. We looked up at each other.

"Static," I said.

"No doubt."

"Thanks for sharing the washer and dryer with me."

"You're welcome. Have we met before?"

"No, I don't believe so."

"What about you? What do you do?" Ginger said as she started putting her clothes into the washer with mine.

"I'm a mathematician. I work with professors and scientists designing experiments and analyzing data to learn why certain things happen."

"What things?"

"All kinds of things. For example, the greater the price difference between the cost of a cesarean birth and the cost of a vaginal birth in a city, the greater the percentage of cesarean births. And congressional districts where Democrats and Republicans spend the most money on elections have higher incidences of demonstrations that turn violent. A lot of work goes into why these things happen and what can be done about them."

"Wow!"

Ginger put detergent into the washer and pushed start. "You want to sit and talk while we wait?" she asked.

"Sure."

"When is your divorce final?"

"In about six weeks."

"And what do you do for fun?"

"This might sound boring, but I play chess."

"What a coincidence, I play chess too."

"We'll have to play sometime."

"Yes, I'm positive we'll play." Ginger continued to talk about chess; the openings she liked, those she didn't, her favorite matches, chess pieces, chess clocks, and more. She continued talking until the washer was done.

We went to move our clothes to the dryer. Ginger apparently had no issue with me touching her things despite the fact they were mostly undergarments.

"I'm playing in a chess tournament this Saturday. Would like you to come with me?" Ginger asked.

"Yes, I'd like that." I had played in tournaments before, so I knew what to expect.

"Great. Why are you looking at me like that?"

"Sorry, it's just your eyeshadow. It looks like it has glitter in it."

Ginger let out a small giggle. "Don't be silly."

She started right up on how to pick the best eyeshadow and the application process. I never realized it could be so involved. Then she moved on to picking the best lipstick color and how to apply it according to the shape of your lips.

"It's interesting, that some women think red lipstick doesn't look good on them, so they never wear it. But any woman can look good in red. You just need the right shade, which can take a while to find. I know it did me."

She continued talking about makeup until the dryer was done. That was fine with me, because it allowed me to continue looking at her face without feeling awkward. When the dryer finished, Ginger realized she was about to be late for a class. We sorted the clothes as fast as we could, and she dashed out of the laundromat.

Later in the day as I was putting away my laundry, I noticed Lisa's pair of pink panties were missing. If I remembered, I'd ask Ginger for them.

I met Ginger at the chess tournament on Saturday and had a good time. I spent most of the time watching Ginger, but I'd walk around and watch other matches too. Ginger won all three of her matches.

"Your rook sacrifice and mate in two—I didn't see that coming. Great move, Ginger."

"Thanks. I like catching people off guard. If I keep playing this well, I should reach the rank of grandmaster within two years."

"That's fantastic. I didn't realize you were that good."

"I'm good at everything, Rocklin." She winked at me.

After I took her to her apartment, she kissed me on the lips and said I brought her good luck. She invited me to do laundry with her the following Saturday and have lunch afterwards. I met her on Saturday.

"Great, Rocklin, you've got a full basket."

"I hope that's okay."

"Sure. I'll get the washer started."

After our laundry finished, we headed to the Acumen Sandwich Shop, across the street from her college. The food was excellent. The shop was owned by a French man and a German woman—husband and wife. Occasionally, if the subject of World War II came up you heard raised voices in French and German, with the French voice referring to Hitler now and then and the German voice referring to the Treaty of Versailles. The patrons got a kick out of it, but the owners, not so much. One of the students had come up with a game to play with the owners that had become very popular. A customer would ask the owners whether a certain person was good or bad. Usually the name was of someone a bit obscure, a name the average person would not know, someone in the French Resistance, a German fighter pilot, the mayor of Lyon, or the highest-ranking Catholic bishop in Germany during the war. The owners loved the game, as it was rare that one of the pair didn't know the name, and they liked showing off to the young know-it-alls. It got to be such an event that the questions were scheduled, and dozens of students would show up, if only to watch.

"Well, what are you going to order today?" I asked Ginger.

"I think I'll order a number eight. It's a French sandwich I've never tried. And I'm always open to new things." There was that wink again.

"I think I'll have a plain ham and cheese."

We placed our orders with the server.

"Ginger, I noticed during the chess tournament last week that you would watch the eyes of your opponent when it was their turn to move."

"That's right. As a fellow chess player, you know any insight can give you an edge. And knowing where on the board your opponent is spending time looking is a clue. That's also why I wear a top with a bit of cleavage. Sometimes it will throw a guy completely off his game, especially if I catch him looking."

"I'll have to remember that."

Ginger smiled and raised her eyebrows.

A loud bong sounded five times, announcing time for the name game. The owners went over to table one. Which student got to choose the name was determined by drawing straws. The name was Virginia Hall. The husband knew the name and the wife did not. After that challenge, our sandwiches arrived.

Ginger invited me to a movie the following Saturday and said she had a special supper planned at her place after the movie. I accepted.

On Saturday we went to see *Valkyrie*. I thought the movie was great despite knowing the ending. Then we went to Ginger's apartment.

"Sit anywhere, Rocklin. Supper will be ready in a minute. I need to change and put supper on the table."

Ginger had mentioned she had a roommate, Penny, who would be out for the evening. She left me in the living room. I walked around the apartment. It was clean and neat. There was a bookcase with books and framed pictures. A sofa, recliner, and rocking chair were spread around the room. In front of the sliding glass door to the patio was a table. It had her medical books and assorted notebooks on it. I went back to the bookcase to look at the books and pictures more closely.

As I was looking at the pictures, I was startled by one. There were five people in the picture, including Ginger. I knew everyone in the picture and one of them was—

"Rocklin, supper is on the table."

Ginger had changed into shorts and a white T-shirt. I didn't ask about the picture. She had fixed gazpacho, which happened to be my favorite dish. Everyone's gazpacho recipe varies a bit, but this tasted like my recipe, without the garlic.

"I got back four of my exams this week."

"How'd you do?"

"Three A's and one B."

"That's great."

"Yes, but it should have been four A's. I've never made less than an A on a final. One of the professors has had it in for me."

"Oh."

"It's because I show her up in class. Well, it doesn't really matter. My grades are good enough for me to get the pick of hospitals for my residency. Most interns end up having to move to another city or state, but I'll be able to stay in town." Ginger winked. "Won't that be great?"

I winked back.

After supper we played a game of chess with strict time limits. Ginger beat me, but I battled well. Then we went over to the sofa, and I remembered to ask about Lisa's panties.

"Oh, Ginger, I've been meaning to ask, do you have my wife's pink panties?"

"Yes."

"Can I have them back?"

"Sure." Lisa stood up and took off her shorts. She was wearing them. "Go ahead, take them."

At that, we heard a key in the door and Penny walked in, oblivious to Ginger's state of dress.

"God, Danny is such a jerk," Penny said as she walked over to us.

Ginger left the room, and Penny stood in front of me continuing her rant. "He knows I don't smoke, and still he gives me a carton of cigarettes and a subscription to *The Southern Review*. What is *The Southern Review*? And who gives their girlfriend a subscription?"

Penny kept on for two or three minutes. Then Ginger walked back into the room—dressed. She was dismayed; Penny was oblivious.

Penny plopped onto the sofa. "How are you doing? I didn't interrupt anything, did I?"

"No, we just finished our chess game. Rocklin was getting ready to go." Ginger looked at me. "Come on. I'll walk you to your car."

We left.

"Sorry about Penny. She's a bit of a moron and only thinks about herself."

"No problem."

On the landing between the first and second floors, Ginger pushed me against the wall, wanting a kiss. Five minutes later, we exited the building and walked to my car.

"How would you like to go bowling Wednesday morning?" Ginger asked.

I had told her earlier I was going to be off the entire week.

"I don't have classes, and if we get there early, say nine thirty, no one else will be bowling."

"Sure." We arranged to meet at the bowling lanes.

I arrived at the bowling alley a minute before Ginger, and we walked in together. At the far end of the alley were four young women bowling on Lane Two.

"We'd like a lane," Ginger said.

"Sure," said the clerk. "I'll put you on Lane Thirty-eight. Do you need to rent shoes?"

"Yes, we need shoes, but can you put us closer to the women on Lane Two?" Ginger continued.

"Closer?"

"Yes."

"Okay, how about Lane Eight?"

"What about Lane Four?"

"Lane Four, when you have all this space?"

"Yes."

"Okay, Lane Four it is."

I was puzzled that Ginger wanted to be so close to the other bowlers.

After we got our shoes and picked out our bowling balls, we went to Lane Four. It turned out that Ginger knew all four of the other women bowling, and one of them was Langley. I spoke to Langley briefly and asked that she not mention to Lisa about seeing me. She nodded. I noticed Ginger scowled briefly. Ginger seemed to hang all over me through the first five frames. Then when the other women left, Ginger stopped being so touchy-feely.

Ginger bowled a 222, while I bowled a 160.

"You bowled great today. I've been bowling on and off for about ten years. How long have you been bowling?" I asked.

"First time."

"What? No way. First time, and you bowled 222. That's extraordinary."

"I watched a YouTube video and practiced in my mind."

I had read that practicing a sport in your mind is as productive as actual practice, but still, why would she want to go bowling if she had never bowled before?

Ginger invited me to go to the state fair with her the following weekend.

When I picked her up to head to the fair, Ginger looked ready. Flip-flops with toenails painted bright green, a medium-length pleated green skirt, and a fitted green top to finish it off. Her lips and eyes looked alluring, as usual.

"Rocklin, they've got a new ride this year I want to try."

"What is it?"

"It's a huge Ferris wheel with large pods that hold ten people each. You stand because there are no seats."

"Ah . . . I don't do well with heights."

"You'll be fine. The pods are enclosed. You can't fall out. Besides, I know a kissing game we can play if you start feeling out of sorts."

"I don't think kissing will be enough."

"This kissing will be. You close your eyes, then when we

kiss, with our tongues we spell out words on the other's tongue, and we try to figure out the word."

"Where in the world did you get that idea?"

"Psych class. We are studying vertigo, and each student had to come up with a way to combat it. The kissing game is what I came up with. I got extra credit for the most creative idea. If we try it and it works, I'll get more credit."

"Oh, brother."

Even though we didn't try the kissing game because of the commotion, Ginger still got extra credit because of what happened. When the Ferris wheel pod we were in was about halfway to the top, a man lost control. He ran over to the plastic window and began screaming, "Let me out! Let me out!" while clawing at the window. Everyone stood frozen. Within seconds Ginger pulled off her skirt and threw it over the man's head so he could not see. He stopped screaming and plopped on the floor of the pod, seemingly calm. The other folks let out a sigh of relief seeing that the unorthodox solution worked. Ginger stood there in her bright green panties, gently holding her skirt on the man's head.

Ginger looked at me and said, "This was my second idea."

After we got off the Ferris wheel, the other passengers gave Ginger a round of applause. She was glowing, turned to me, and gave me a sweet kiss.

I took her back to her apartment to say good night.

"Rocklin, I've got another chess tournament on Saturday. I thought maybe you'd come. You bring me good luck."

"Ginger, I'd love to, but I have a prior commitment."

"Oh."

"Lisa, my wife, about to be ex-wife, is having a family reunion, a cookout, and I promised her I would come. She wants me to say bye to some folks I might not see again."

"I see."

"You understand."

"Of course." In spite of her words, her face told a different story. "Wait a second, I'll be right back."

When she came back, she had a pocket notebook and a pen. "Here, take these. And do me a teensy-weensy favor."

"Sure."

"Anytime you talk with Lisa during the reunion, make a note in the notebook and write down what you both said."

"Okay." The request seemed a bit odd, but Ginger didn't have to be worried about Lisa. If anything, she should have been concerned about Langley.

At the reunion Lisa and I reminisced on and off about the good times, the sweet times; there were some. I didn't write in the notebook. Later, I would make up a few things to write down. I wandered all over, talking to folks, making sure I said bye to the relatives who lived out of state. Most were cordial, but I knew Lisa's dad, Charlie, was not happy with me. I saw him break the five-second rule—he dropped a burger off the grill, and it sat on the ground for ten seconds before he plopped it back on. I don't think you're even allowed five seconds if it happens in the backyard and you've had dogs roaming around earlier.

Lisa and I were sitting on the swing talking.

"Lisa, do you know Ginger Raines?"

"Ginger Raines?"

"Yes. I saw you and a couple of your friends in a picture with her. I happened to meet her at the laundromat, and we've been going out."

"You and Ginger haven't . . . ah . . . well . . . I mean . . ."

"No, no. Although her motor runs hot, I have deflected her amorous intentions. She's not affectionate though."

"She's amorous but not affectionate. How can that be?"

"They're different things, Lisa."

"If you say so. I don't think you just ran into Ginger. She wanted to run into you. I don't hang around with her anymore because she used to ask me questions about you. Personal questions."

"Really?"

"Yes, she's self-absorbed. She covets things, especially men it seems."

Considering that Lisa was prone to jealousy, I didn't take her too seriously.

Just then Charlie walked over. He put his hand on my shoulder and said the code enforcement officer was in the front yard and asked me to placate him until he was finished with the burgers. I doubted he would finish with the burgers. He probably hoped I'd pull out my wallet and take care of any fine. Then I remembered that the code enforcement officer was a drinking buddy of Charlie's. I asked, "Why the big deal?"

"Nah," Charlie said, "This is a new guy. He takes the job a bit too seriously, from what I understand."

I walked around to the front. Maybe I could insult the guy and get the fine increased. A sly grin spread across my face.

The code enforcer was wearing tan coveralls with a badge that said My Name is Art.

"Hello, Art," I said in an especially friendly tone.

"We have a variety of violations here don't you know?" Art replied with no tone at all, holding a clipboard and marking items with a red marker.

"Like what?"

"A sofa on the front porch, too many cars parked on the street; too high a decibel level, creating *The Sound and the Fury,* so to speak; too many dogs on the property; one vehicle with Mississippi plates . . . but I'll give you a pass on the re-frigerator on the side of the house, since it's covered by ivy."

With furrowed brows I said, "Mississippi plates?"

Art laughed. "Code enforcement humor."

"*The Sound and the Fury.* You a Faulkner fan?" I asked.

Art stopped marking the paper on the clipboard and looked up at me. "You one too?"

"A great writer, no question, but I prefer shorter fiction, Raymond Carver, Alice Munro, George Singleton, Raymond Chandler, the short stories of Ray Bradbury."

"This your place?"

"No, no, it belongs to my . . . ah . . . a guy I know. He's hav-ing a little get-together."

"It's getting a bit hot in my coveralls. You don't mind, do you?" Art asked as the zipper on the front of the coveralls started going down.

"Knock yourself out."

As Art was taking off the coveralls, I saw why she was sup-posed to wear them. She wore hip-hugging blue jeans and a fitted white T-shirt that said *Wisdom is Gender Neutral.*

"These violations need to be rectified in the next two hours."

"Well, there's a better chance of Bob Dylan winning the Nobel Prize in literature."

We both looked at each other and then burst out laughing.

"What's your name?" Art asked.

"Rocklin Evans."

"Have you always enjoyed reading, Rocklin?"

"Actually, no. I despised all the reading I had to do during the four years of high school English."

"Why?"

"With my attention span, I would get bored well before the

end of the book. Then after we finished, we would spend a week or two discussing what the author meant, which was a waste of time."

"How so?"

"You're not going to know what an author meant unless the author tells you. One of the books we read was by a famous author who was still living. The class divided into two groups about the meaning of a certain chapter. The teacher wrote the author and asked which interpretation was correct. The author wrote back and said sometimes a story is just a story."

"Oh, I love it."

We talked for a few more minutes, and Art gave me the code enforcement fine to give Charlie. I put it in the mailbox.

I headed back to the reunion to review Langley's latest edits of my story with her. We met up in Charlie's office. Sitting side by side, we reviewed the marked-up story. The red marks were grammar errors, while the green marks indicated a story problem: flow, emotion, confusion, and the like. At one point Langley's hand was on mine, our faces only inches apart. Langley stop talking; I thought she would kiss me. Wishful thinking, maybe. She got up and went to Charlie's desk and sat down.

"This girl, Ginger. Do you like her?" Langley said as she ran her fingers back and forth over Charlie's phone.

"She's okay."

"But she's not someone you can envision marrying, is she?"

"No, no she's not."

"Do you know anyone you might want to marry?"

"Perhaps." I couldn't believe the timing of her question, when I had been thinking about just that—marrying someone.

"Good," Langley said with a grin. "I thought so."

I continued to see Langley after the divorce. Over the

following year, she and I spent a lot of time together. After all, she needed to edit my stories.

While a radio played in the background, I was married to my fiancée by the clerk at city hall. Just as the clerk pronounced us man and wife, the radio announcer said that Bob Dylan had won this year's Nobel Prize in literature. Art and I looked at each other and burst out laughing just before we kissed. It was only later that I learned Art and Langley were friends and that Art's visit to Charlie's had been arranged. Langley, being so perceptive, believed that Art and I would be a perfect match. She was right.

The End

7

Rent What?

My mother thought it was wrong. My former girlfriend, Elise, thought it was a bad idea. I should never have told them. But the idea was brilliant. It would keep me from failing my final class, allowing me to graduate from law school at last. I was approaching my sixth year in school, and I wanted it and my crummy job at the bowling alley to end. I had already passed the bar exam and had an undergraduate degree in accounting and a job as a forensic investigator with the Securities and Exchange Commission lined up conditional on my graduating. I didn't see how it could go wrong. After all, Ms. Highlander was known for tutoring students before an exam and being lenient with grading if the student loved dogs as much as she.

My six tutoring sessions with Ms. Highlander were scheduled over three weeks, so I arranged to rent a dog from C. F. for the duration. I saw the ad for *Rent a Pet* in the local paper. I don't know that C. F. was shady, but a few things were odd. You didn't know his name, just C. F. His business was cash only, and he ran it out of a store two doors down from the county animal shelter. The store was unlabeled except for the number 511, and all the business was conducted through the back door. I called C. F. to find out what I needed to do and the cost.

"Hello, C. F?"

"Speaking."

"I need to rent a dog for three weeks."

"Sure, come by tomorrow evening at six, and you can pick up your dog."

"How much?"

"Six hundred dollars."

"Okay." I knew it might be high, but how many places let you rent a dog? "When can I come by and pick out the dog?"

"Pick it out, no. We give you the dog. You don't pick it out."

"But I have certain requirements."

"Look, we're not set up to do that. And you're not marrying it for God's sake. You're just renting it. It shouldn't matter."

I was taken aback. I knew little about dogs, but I knew I didn't want a squirt of a dog or a dog as big as a horse.

"One hundred dollars extra if I can pick out the dog."

I heard a sigh. "Just tell me what you want, and I'll get as close as I can."

That seemed fair enough. "I don't want a small dog or a large dog. I would say between medium and large. A medium-large dog, if you will."

"That's it?"

"Yes."

"Okay, I'll get as close as I can. See you tomorrow. Cash only, park around back and come to the back door."

"Sure. Bye." Easy enough.

To get ready for the dog, I bought a few supplies, such as a bowl, plastic bone, and the like. I also borrowed a book, *Raising Your Dog,* which I read. Well, I read parts of it and skimmed the rest.

The next day at six o'clock, I was at C. F.'s store. I knocked on the back door. I heard it unlock. C. F. came out, looked around, and told me to come in.

"You got the money?"

"Yep, here you go."

"Okay, here's your dog." He handed me the leash with a medium-large dog at the end of it. The dog was mostly light brown with a few white spots mixed in.

"What's his name?"

"What do you think a dog should be named?"

"I don't know. Spot."

"What a coincidence; that's the dog's name, Spot."

"Does he come when you call him?"

"If he's in the mood."

I frowned. "Does he know commands?"

"Sure. Roll over."

At that, Spot sat.

"He's still learning."

"What kind of dog is he?"

"A mix."

"A mix of what?"

"A mix of a mix. Does it matter?"

I shrugged. "I'll bring him back in three weeks."

"Call first, and we'll arrange the return."

"Okay."

Spot appeared keen on having a new owner. He seemed to have a friendly attitude toward me and followed me when I left as if he didn't need the leash.

When we got home, I gave Spot some water and took him for a walk. I petted him a lot that evening so he'd get used to me. My first tutoring session was the next morning at ten at

Ms. Highlander's home. The next day I gave Spot some water and food and took him for a walk. Then we headed to my session.

I had Spot on the leash as I rang the doorbell. When Ms. Highlander answered the door, I scarcely recognized her. In class she wore long dresses with her hair in a bun and looked like a thirty-eight-year-old law professor, but not now. She looked ten years younger. Her long black hair flowed over her shoulders, and she was wearing a white T-shirt, orange shorts, and orange flip-flops.

"Good morning, Ms. Highlander."

"Stuart, outside of class it's Jean, please. I see you brought a buddy. What's his name?"

"Spot."

Jean reached down and gave Spot a vigorous rub about his head and side. "Come in."

We walked to the kitchen. Jean took the leash from me and untethered Spot.

"You're not going to leave Spot tied up?"

"No, of course not. He'll be fine in the kitchen. I'll close the door, and we can study uninterrupted in the den."

Jean gave Spot a bowl of water. "There, Spot can have a drink and relax. My dogs are in the backyard, so he won't be bothered."

Jean and I went to the den and sat on opposite sides of a round glass table. A stack of law books sat on a rolling wooden cart next to the table. The table was near the sliding glass door to the backyard, so we had plenty of light. We started reviewing court cases involving free speech. Ms. Highlander also had commentaries on free speech by the Founding Fathers marked in various books.

I had difficulty concentrating. My attention was divided

between wondering what Spot was doing and whether Ms. Highlander was married. We were two rooms away from the kitchen.

"Stuart, you seem distracted. Is something wrong?"

"No, no. I'm just tired and worried about the exam."

"Please, don't even think about the exam. Your work has always been above average. I'll be back in a few minutes. I need to unlock the back gate for the lawn service."

I knew it was risky, but I headed to the kitchen. Spot was up on the breakfast bar, his head in a large bowl, licking it. Then he lifted a leg and relieved himself in the bowl. I stood there, mouth agape. When he finished, I put him on the floor, poured the bowl's contents down the sink, grabbed some dish-washing liquid, swished the soap and water in the bowl, and rinsed. I did this several times, but the smell remained. I was scrubbing the bowl with a soapy sponge when Ms. Highlander walked in.

"Stuart, what in heaven's name are you doing?"

"Washing dishes. I always wash dishes when I'm nervous."

"Maybe you should come over more often."

I looked at Ms. Highlander with a startled expression.

"I'm kidding, Stuart. That could come in handy when you're married, though. Stop, and let's get back to studying."

After Ms. Highlander turned around, I squeezed the sponge and threw it in the trash.

We studied for two more hours, and I wondered if I needed to bring Spot with me in the future now that Ms. Highlander knew I owned a dog. It would sure make things easier.

"Stuart, I think that's it for today."

As we were standing at the door saying goodbye, Ms. Highlander reached down and rubbed Spot vigorously again.

"Be sure to bring Spot next time. There is something about

him. He seems special in some way. What breed is he?"

"A mix."

"A mix of what?"

"I . . . I don't know. I guess I didn't think to ask. I had already fallen for him, so it didn't matter to me." Oh, gosh. That was so syrupy, I cringed inside.

"Oh, that's so sweet." Ms. Highlander gave me a hug. I stiffened at the surprise, growing more and more embarrassed until she let go.

"Bye, Ms. Highlander. See you again in a few days."

"Bye, Stuart."

I think she realized my calling her Jean made me nervous.

On the way back to my apartment, I felt better. I had made it through one session and would have to steel myself for the other five.

The next day I had no classes, so I went to the bank to get some cash, bringing Spot with me for his walk. The ATM was out of order, and a note taped on the screen directed me inside.

Inside the bank were several dozen people. I had never seen the lobby so busy, and nearly every customer had a dog.

"Excuse me," I said to a young woman. "Why do so many customers have dogs?"

"Aren't you here to open a new account too?"

"New account, no. I already have an account."

"Well, if you're a dog owner and open a new account, the bank will deposit five hundred dollars in it after ninety days."

"Oh, thanks." I still needed cash, so I got in line.

For some reason Spot was a bit more unruly than usual, as if he'd had too much coffee. He was trying to pull me all around, sniffing people and other dogs. Kinda like he had to find a killer and only had one minute to do it. I had a time keeping him away from other dogs and customers.

"Excuse me," a mature gentleman said to me. "Perhaps you should wait outside, since you're one of *those* people."

"Those people?"

"A person who doesn't believe in neutering his dog, thinking it diminishes its dogness."

"Dogness—I'm pretty sure that's not a word."

The man gave me a stern look and turned away.

Suddenly, all the dogs in the bank started barking, howling, and jumping around, Spot more than the others. I can't be sure of the time, but about thirty seconds later, the bank's alarm went off, and the doors automatically shut. About thirty seconds after that, most of the dogs calmed down. Five minutes later, the police arrived, the alarm was shut off, and the doors were opened to let the police in. Naturally, none of the customers were allowed to leave. Just when it appeared we would be allowed to go, the police discovered that $25,000 dollars was missing, and a dog whistle had been found in one of the trash cans. We were told to have a seat and wait to be interviewed and searched. Most of the interviews were conducted in the lobby, but I was invited to a conference room by the detective who appeared to be in charge. A second officer was inside and a third officer stood outside the door. Both the door and the walls of the conference room were made of glass, and as I sat down, I could see that some of the customers in the lobby were being allowed to leave.

The second officer took Spot's leash.

"What is your name?" the detective asked me.

"Stuart Widmark."

"Why are you here today?"

"I needed some cash."

"Mr. Widmark, someone took advantage of all the dogs in

the bank today by using a dog whistle to create confusion and rob the bank."

"I didn't do it."

"In our interviews, several customers indicated you had trouble controlling your dog, as if you have little experience with dogs."

"He's a new dog. I'm a new dog owner."

"Where'd you get the dog?"

"From . . . why does that matter?"

"Mr. Widmark, we need to confirm your story. And your dog isn't neutered, so he's overly aggressive. You needed to create as much disruption as possible."

"Detective . . . I'm sorry, I didn't get your name."

"Highlander."

That was interesting.

"Detective Highlander, you're blaming testosterone only because that's what your veterinarian told you. You're begging the question. Testosterone doesn't necessarily result in increased aggressive behavior unless there is already a propensity for aggression."

Detective Highlander let out a bellowing laugh. "You—a new dog owner—are going to lecture me on neutered dogs? I think not."

Debating with a man who could throw you in jail didn't seem like a good idea. I didn't know what to do next when someone knocked on the door. It was Ms. Highlander. The detective waved her in.

"Simon, what are you doing with Stuart?"

"He's the primary person of interest in the bank robbery."

"He's no bank robber. I know him. He is one of my students."

Ms. Highlander pulled up a chair next to me and sat.

"Give me your hand—your left hand, Stuart."

"Jean, is this necessary?" asked the detective.

"It will save you a lot of time. You know that."

Ms. Highlander held my hand. Actually, she was holding my left wrist. She looked directly into my eyes.

"Stuart, you need to be completely honest with me. I'll be able to tell if you're lying. Okay?"

"Yes, of course.

"Did the goodbye yesterday embarrass you?"

The hug and my reaction popped into my mind, and I said, "Yes."

She smiled faintly and waited about fifteen seconds. "Okay, take a few deep breaths. Did you rob this bank today?"

"No."

She waited another fifteen seconds and stood up. "Based on his pulse and eye dilation, Stuart is telling the truth. Happy now?"

"Mr. Widmark, you're free to go. Give the officer your address before you go. Sis, I guess I should thank you for saving me time."

"What are sisters for?"

As Spot and I walked home, I kept replaying events at the bank and thought of possible ramifications. My mind ran wild counting all the ways Ms. Highlander might find out I had rented Spot. I was doubting my decision.

On Saturday morning I got up and walked Spot. It was seventy degrees with a slight breeze, so I decided to walk the few blocks to the city park.

Spot and I passed a woman walking her cat on a leash. As we got closer to the park, I saw more people—mostly women—with their cats on leashes. I started getting scowls, so much so that I took a selfie to be sure something wasn't on my face that shouldn't be, but no, there wasn't anything. Spot didn't seem bothered by the cats.

When we reached the park, there were women and cats aplenty. Many of the women wore blue T-shirts with SAD emblazoned across the front. My first thought was perhaps it might have to do with some female condition. I remembered my father telling me if I got married to read up on menopause when my wife reached her late forties. He implied that knowing about menopause beforehand would help me immensely, especially if my wife owned a gun. I was oblivious.

When I looked more closely at the T-shirts, I saw that *Stop Aggressive Dogs* was written beneath SAD. I remembered what my mom had told me: a political divide was growing in the city council elections between dog lovers and cat lovers. Questions about a candidate's position on cats and dogs were the most frequently asked at political events. The demands on each side seemed bizarre: no cats outside without a leash, dogs walked only between certain hours, cat and dog free zones in the city. After the elections, both sides denounced each other with accusations of voter fraud. The main accusation: out-of-town residents moving in with relatives prior to the election. I didn't stay long in the park.

Finally, Ms. Highlander and I met for my final tutoring session. We took Spot to the kitchen as usual. I was glad the dog rental was nearly over and had already arranged to return Spot the next day. Ms. Highlander and I went to the den as usual.

"Stuart, my sister Lillian might interrupt us a few times. She will be helping me prepare for a dinner party later today."

"Okay."

About thirty minutes later, Lillian popped her head into the den. "Jean, I'm finally here. I'll set up the dining room and then get started in the kitchen."

"Okay. Lillian, this is one of my students, Stuart. Stuart, my sister, Lillian."

Lillian came over to shake my hand. "Nice to meet you, Stuart."

"Likewise."

Lillian left the room.

"What about Spot? Will he be in Lillian's way?"

"No. Lillian's a dog lover too. If she needs to, she will put him in the laundry room."

A bit later Lillian rushed into the den with a smile a mile wide almost shouting.

"Jean, you darling sister! Why didn't you tell me?"

"Tell you? Tell you what?"

"That you found Tops! He's in the kitchen, you dazzling sister—missing the past three weeks, and you found him. How did you ever . . . don't you remember? Animal Control told me they had a dog matching Tops's description, but when I got there, there was no such dog."

Uh-oh!

"Lillian, I never got to see Tops after you bought him. How could I have known what . . ." Ms. Highlander stopped and looked at me. "Oh . . . my!" She turned toward her sister. "Lillian, go back to the kitchen. Let me finish with Stuart. I'll explain later."

"Okay." Lillian rushed back to the kitchen after giving Ms. Highlander a hug.

"Stuart, do I need to hold your wrist again?"

"No, ma'am."

"What about Spot?"

"I knew you loved dogs, so I rented him."

"Rented from whom?"

"C. F."

"C. F. What's his name?"

"That's all the name he gave me."

"Did you know C. F. was taking dogs from the shelter?"

"Not at the time but it's obvious now."

"I see. What do you suppose C. F. will do when you don't return Spot?"

"Nothing."

"Indeed."

"I guess this means no more hugs."

Ms. Highlander burst out laughing. "Just one more, for *finding* Tops. How about that?"

"How about that indeed."

The End

8

I Won the Lottery

I stood in line waiting to buy milk, but my buying the lottery ticket was a second thought. Despite the long line, I kept coming back to this Jiffy Mart because it was close to my house. Sergey and Natalia, the owners who immigrated from Russia, thought a checkout line that didn't wrap around the block three times was an express checkout, so they never opened more than one register. Because of what happened to me after I bought the lottery ticket, I would never buy another one, even if you told me I'd win—especially if you told me I'd win.

Why? Because I knew the truth, a rare commodity. Just this past week I'd read that Jack Lord's eyes were blue; Jack Lord's eyes were brown; dark roast coffee has more antioxidants than regular coffee; dark roast coffee has fewer antioxidants than regular coffee.

I bought the ticket because the lottery was at $1.2 billion, and I had been fantasizing about all the wonderful things I could do with the money.

That night I double-checked the numbers. Yep, I had the winning numbers. I put the ticket in a small food container and put the container in the freezer behind the scallops and brussels sprouts. My mind raced: buy a new house, buy a new car, retire, give money to worthy causes, collect things (I didn't know what), buy a second home—maybe in Monte Carlo—and travel the world. I could have butlers and cooks and maids and servants. I, a twenty-eight-year-old, unmarried, high school English teacher, had won the lottery.

And a girlfriend, I was on the lookout for a girlfriend since Jenna dumped me two months ago. We had dated for six weeks before we broke up. One day when she dropped by to pick me up, I wasn't ready, so she came inside to wait. She hadn't been in my house before.

As I was coming down the stairs to join her, she asked, "Are all the walls in your house white?"

"Yes."

"Bad karma, very bad. I'm getting negative waves here."

What in the sam hill. Jenna was a financial analyst for Goldman Sachs, and she was asking about white paint and talking about karma and negative waves. She sounded like a hippie chick. This was the first portent of something gone wrong. Up to then our conversations had been highbrow.

"Sorry, John, but whenever I've gotten negative waves this strong, the relationship has never worked. I'm sorry, bye."

After thinking it over, I wasn't sure whether it was the white walls or the fact that I had left my pay stub on the counter. The house was more than I could afford to buy, but not more than I could afford to own; it was inherited. I bet those white walls have pretty good karma now.

I decided to wait two months before claiming the winnings. It was well known that people who took their lottery winnings right away did foolish things such as buying a Maserati that was totaled in a week, having a home built in Colorado with a panoramic view on a mountain that was so hard to get to that the owner only went once, and making donations to a Nigerian charity for crippled children—donations funneled to a Chinese rock band that toured the world—a rock band of hackers that downloaded bookoodles of technology secrets from companies in each country and passed them on to the China Republic Administration of State Security, CRASS for short, an arm of the communist party.

I was determined to have a plan. The law had been changed to protect the privacy of individuals by making it illegal for lottery officials—or anyone—to disclose the names of winners. Still, I was concerned people would find out. If that happened, there would be an avalanche of folks wanting my money for everything imaginable. I copied the lottery ticket and spent the rest of the night pondering where to hide the original ticket for the next two months. I decided to put it in my safe-deposit box.

While I was driving to the bank the next day, I had a feeling of foreboding. As I was about to enter the bank, a black cat ran in front of me, the security guard in the bank failed to say "God bless you" when I sneezed, and the calendar at the safe deposit box check-in displayed Friday the thirteenth. And despite my believing all those things were appalling superstitions, I decided to put the copy in the safe-deposit box and the original elsewhere. After finishing at the bank, I picked up some fertilizer for the lawn, went by Tom's Used Book Store, and ran one more errand—to hide the ticket. I spent the rest of the day watching reruns of *Hawaii Five-O* (the original) to distract myself. I had started out watching reruns of the original *Twilight Zone,* but stopped after two episodes, as I started imagining that my winning the lottery was an episode somehow.

The next day I went to the post office before going to pick up a few groceries at Walmart. While I was walking to the car with my groceries, a white van screeched to a halt next to me. Three men jumped out, grabbed me, held a cloth over my face, and threw me into the van.

When I came to, I found myself tied to a metal chair bolted to the floor in a large, well-lit room. The walls appeared to be thick sheet metal, and I only saw one door. A camera above the door was trained on me.

A few feet in front of me were two long folding tables, side by side. One had stacks of hundred-dollar bills and American Eagle Gold coins. The other table was strewn with scalpels, rubber gloves, and syringes, which made me feel queasy.

Could I be dreaming? Why would anyone kidnap me? And I had not told a soul about winning the lottery. I hadn't even uttered the words aloud to myself that I had won. Perhaps it was a case of mistaken identity.

Finally, I heard the door unlock. Three men in navy blue suits, white shirts, Allen Edmonds shoes, and blue ties marched into the room. Two of them took up positions on each side of the door. The third man—medium height, stocky, bald, with the face of a mob enforcer—grabbed a folding chair, casually placed it in front of me, and sat down.

"I'll get to the point, John. You have something that my friends and I want. We want it badly, and we'll pay you for it. And as you can see, you're in no position to dicker. There's ten million dollars in cash and gold on that table. You can walk out of here with it. It's tax-free, unlike lottery winnings. We'll even help you load it into your car. Given your modest tastes, you can live nicely on ten million. After you tell us where the lottery ticket is and we retrieve it, we'll let you go. You can keep the ten million."

My mouth dropped open in astonishment.

"Oh, you're surprised. I can understand that, but let's move on. Where is the ticket, John?"

I was baffled, so I played dumb. "You've made a terrible mistake. I don't know what you're talking about."

Mr. Enforcer leaned forward and looked at me hard. Speaking slowly and softly, the man said, "John, we've seen the copy of your winning ticket. You know, the copy in your safe-deposit box."

My mind went blank; I felt faint. I couldn't comprehend how these men . . .

"You're no dummy, John. You should know that I work for a first-class organization. We've been able to access your safe-deposit box. We've searched your house and your car. We started following you soon after you won. That woman who bumped into you at the post office, she took your wallet to see if the ticket was there. The bum who stumbled into you a few minutes later, he put it back."

I was mystified, but I started getting angry: *How dare they!* Having grown up on reruns of *Have Gun–Will Travel, Gunsmoke, Bonanza,* and *Daniel Boone,* I believed you always did the right thing, regardless.

"You have to be impressed with our organization, John. Even the FBI doesn't know about us. You're not getting any help. There's no one to call. No one would believe you anyway. On the other table, John, we have . . . shall we say a less generous table. I don't even like looking at it; it distresses me terribly. I'm sure you can imagine what a cruel person could do with those instruments. Is it worth it when you could have ten million tax-free?"

I wasn't afraid of dying, never have been oddly enough, so my anger took over. "I'm going to die no matter what. You mobsters, or hackers, or whoever you are, I'm sure you can make me disappear. I believe in fairness; I believe in justice; I believe in economic equality; I believe evil should be punished. I'm a Bernie voter for God's sake, so I'm not inclined to help you."

At the mention of the name Bernie, one of the men at the door chuckled. *Mr. Enforcer* turned and gave the chuckling man a stern look, and he fell silent.

"Yes, we could kill you, John, but we're not going to. Why? Because we're not allowed to. But now that I think about it, if you're dead, in all likelihood that would accomplish our goal. Still, I couldn't be absolutely sure unless I had the ticket."

I didn't see how my being dead would help if I hadn't given them the ticket.

"But let's not dwell on worst-case, John. Being a Bernie voter, you understand the lottery winnings would put you in the top one percent. Why, that amount of money would put you in the top one percent of the top one percent. Is that fair when the money could help so many others?"

"Don't make me laugh," I said in a feisty manner. "You mean help yourself."

"This lottery money won't help me, John. We're trying to solve a problem here: poverty. After all, the problem isn't that people have different amounts—income inequality—it's that some people don't have enough. This lottery money would help widows, the homeless, the unemployed, and thousands of others living in poverty. You have to believe me on this, John. Giving us the ticket would change people's lives. Think of us as modern-day Robin Hoods. Is that so difficult?"

"You expect me to believe that?" I snapped.

"Yes, I do. Why? Because it's the truth, and I've given you ten million reasons to believe it. What more do you want?

You'll come out of the deal with ten million dollars and a clear conscience. Is that an arrangement anyone would walk away from? I think not, especially considering the consequences of not taking the deal.

"Here's what you don't understand, John. We don't want the ticket to cash it; we want to *destroy* it."

"Hah! You think I just fell off the turnip truck?"

"John, stop and think for a second. Why was the law changed to prevent the disclosure of the winner's name? The government announces someone won, a person who doesn't exist, and the government keeps the money—all of it. I work for the government, John. Our computer systems record every number chosen when a lottery ticket is sold. Then the computer picks the winning numbers, numbers no one picked. However, because of a power surge, the numbers you picked weren't reported to the command center.

"The lottery is a tax, John. Every United States senator knows about this program. The Senate approved it—one hundred to zero. You know what that means? You know who voted for the tax, John?"

My eyebrows went up, my eyes wide. "Not—"

"Should I say it, John? Should I? Bernie! Bernie!

"The government helps people, John. Being a Bernie voter, you understand the government needs money. So, what's the best way for the government to get money? Tax the rich? No, no, John, that's not the answer. Why? Have you seen any of the movies Ronald Reagan made in the forties and fifties? They're great movies, John, great. Bernie loves them too by the way. They're stories with a moral, and his acting was superb.

"But here's the thing: federal income tax rates back then were as high as ninety percent. Ninety percent! And that doesn't include state taxes. Reagan lived in California, a state with its own high tax rates too. Reagan didn't make more than two pictures a year because everything he'd earn after that would have gone to the government.

"Thus, civilization—I'm not joking here, John—misses out on dozens of Reagan movies that never get made because Reagan isn't going to work for free; who would? You *can* tax the rich too much.

"What then? Do we tax the poor? Oh, no, John. That's the problem we're trying to solve. The poor need every penny and more. Like my great-aunt Minnie. Poor Aunt Minnie. Her husband had a government-sponsored 403(b) retirement plan, but when he died, his beneficiary was some trollop. But if her husband had worked for a corporation, not the government, Aunt Minnie would have inherited the money. The government lets government employees leave their money to anyone, but the government requires that corporation employees leave their retirement money to their spouses. Is that fair to my Aunt Minnie? No. The government needs to make it up to her; it needs to make up for its stupid rules that put her in poverty."

My anger softened a tad. Being a schoolteacher, I had a 403(b) plan, and I knew what he said was true. Wives—spouses, I should say—get the short end of the deal.

Mr. Enforcer continued, "But to help Aunt Minnie, the government needs money. Aunt Minnie is supposed to take five different medications each day, but she doesn't. She can't afford to. She buys one pill at a time when money permits. Should anyone have to live like that in this country, John? This money, this lottery money, would allow Congress to expand prescription drug coverage to everyone living in poverty. You want to tell Aunt Minnie she can't get her meds because you're greedy?

"You see, John, ethics is on our side. We're helping the poor, not the one percent.

So, where's the ticket, John?"

The End

9

The Woman on the Bed

Mike invited me to visit him upstate for the weekend. I accepted, suspecting he wanted to check on me like everyone else. I had not wanted to retire; I had to. Had it been traumatic? Yes, but you have to keep moving forward. What else is there?

There was going to be a party at the Clarks' place, a well-to-do family, and Mike was invited to attend with a guest. The party was going to be small—twenty to twenty-five people. Mike casually mentioned that I might take a fancy to one of the guests, Lisa, and at least one book publisher was invited. I was ambivalent about both the woman and the publisher. But now that I had more time, I'd been going to parties partly to show people, *Don't worry*; *I'm doing fine*. I'm glad I went, despite what happened.

Mike told me the party would be held around the backyard pool, but it wasn't intended to be a pool party—not with all the guests over forty. The projected high temperature was sixty-nine degrees with a breeze. I wore shorts and a T-shirt. I didn't pack my swim trunks; I wasn't interested in swimming.

I arrived about 11 a.m. Saturday, and Mike met me at the

train station. He was more helpful than he needed to be, running around getting my bags and checking on my return ticket for Sunday evening. But that was Mike's style. The drive to the Clarks' would take about forty-five minutes.

"Johnny, I'm glad you came up."

"Yeah, well, I thought you might be trying to mother me, but I decided to come anyway."

"Nah, nothing like that. The Clarks know a lot of people—book publishers, for example. And as I said, one will be at the party. I still think you should write a book about your thirty years with the NYPD. You have plenty of intriguing stories. You could make some good money. And besides, with you being the most—"

"Me—write a book? You're kidding," I interrupted with a derisive snort.

"Look, Johnny, with the gossip that's going around about you, your publishing window will probably close soon. I don't believe a word of the buzz, not about you. But if people say something often enough, people start to believe it. You're still young enough that you need to keep your opportunities open. That won't happen if you get dragged through the mud."

"Mike, you know what it's like being a cop. Rumors are everywhere. The rumor that I was on the take reached its crescendo when Dean Winter from the *Gazette* saw me having lunch with Vinny Tuskadero at the Gardens."

"Yeah, I know how the press can make something out of nothing. But Vinny, the murderer, you could only send up the river for extortion, not murder. He's free now and running the business, and the two of you seemed pretty cozy. Then you had lunch with him at the Gardens, the most expensive restaurant in New York. People are bound to talk."

"Vinny's not running the business. He told me he wasn't,

and I believe him. He's been honest with me ever since I saved his son from being kidnapped by Louie Snap. He shows me a certain amount of respect now."

"Yeah, I remember the headline, Cop Saves Mobster's Son From Kidnapping in Blazing Shootout. You, with only your Smith and Wesson revolver, against five bad guys with semi-automatics. Too bad Vinny isn't honest in court too.

"But enough of that, let's talk about the party. First, about the layout in the backyard, if you can call it a backyard. The pool is close to the house. Beyond the pool are five acres of shaded gardens. The whole area is lined with trees, and stone paths meander throughout. It's nice this time of year, especially with the breeze carrying the scent of roses and blue cloud calamint. And there are three small bungalows mixed in, all with private bathrooms. When you're walking though the gardens, it's like you're under the canopy of a rain forest. It's exquisite.

"Here, study this. It's a map of the grounds and the garden. I figured you'd want to know your way around since—"

I cut him off by snapping, "A map of the backyard? You're an idiot."

"No, no, study it and you'll discover that it even has measurements and distances on it." Mike tossed the map onto my lap.

Despite my protests, I studied the map and even had it memorized by the time we arrived.

"I think you'll like Lisa."

Mike didn't see it, but I rolled my eyes at that comment. Still, I was determined to have a good time.

"The Clarks like to keep things informal. They prefer their guests use first names only. They're the salt of the earth, despite the wealth they inherited."

Mike continued with descriptions of the property, the people, and the party etiquette, with comments about Lisa sprinkled in. She was an NYU grad with a degree in literature and library science who was working as a librarian, had never married, and was forty-something.

By the time we arrived, I felt I already knew my way around. We wandered over to a couple of lounge chairs near the pool, and Mike introduced me to the guests as we passed by—first names only.

Mike and I settled into our chairs. People walked by saying hi. I'd nod and say hi back. Soon the host and hostess stopped by. Mike introduced me. Our hostess handed beach towels to both of us as we engaged in the usual small talk—where do you live, are you married, what kind of work do you do. After a few minutes, the hosts excused themselves, as did Mike after seeing a couple he wanted to speak with.

I was soaking up the sun when *the woman* strolled over and introduced herself.

"Hello, you must be Johnny. I'm Lisa."

"Hello," I said, extending my hand. I knew immediately her name wasn't Lisa. She was Vivian Tuskadaro, Vinny's daughter. I had to assume she knew who I was, but I decided to play along in case I was wrong. "Lisa, the NYU graduate and librarian?"

"Oh, so Mike's been giving you the lowdown on me, has he?"

"Naturally."

Lisa plopped down onto Mike's lounge chair.

"You need some sunscreen, Johnny. I've got some. Can I give you a coating?"

"Knock yourself out."

Lisa applied some sunscreen to my arms, neck, and face,

but she didn't take off my sunglasses. Then she asked if I'd coat her. She put the sunscreen in my hand, and I pulled my lounge closer to hers. She was lying on her stomach. She probably had been swimming as she was still wet. When I finished her back, she turned over, took the sunscreen from my hand, and said thanks.

"Mike tells me you've been reading a lot since you retired."

"Yes, both fiction and nonfiction." So, Mike told her I was retired, but did he tell her my name? Although Lisa might not recognize me by sight, she almost certainly knew my name.

"I haven't known Mike long, but I imagine you've known him for a while. Did he work for the NYPD too?"

"Yes, we worked together on and off over the years." So, she did know I worked for the NYPD and my first name. But had Mike told her my last name. I couldn't know for sure until I asked him. If she did know my name, she had to realize I'd recognized her, although we had never met. Several years earlier, I had tried to find her, but couldn't. She'd dropped off the radar. I figured she went deep underground, moved to another country, or was dead. But if she knew who I was, what was she up to?

"What plans do you have for retirement? I mean long term."

"I don't know yet. Mike thinks I should write a book about my time on the force."

"Oh, I wouldn't do that. Exposing secrets, shining a light on people who prefer anonymity—that would make some people very unhappy. They might even come after you—people like Vinny."

Bingo! She *did* know who I was. Mike had no clue he had endangered me by telling her my name. And that gave her the advantage over me, at least for the moment. I didn't know how she felt about Vinny. Maybe she'd kiss me, or maybe she'd kill me.

"You know Vinny?" I asked.

Silence. And naturally, I had no clue what she was thinking.

Suddenly she threw her drink in my face. I know most people saw it, because the talking stopped. If that was it, I got off easy.

Then Lisa slammed her glass onto the patio table and stormed toward the gardens. I casually wiped my face with the beach towel. Since I knew the garden's layout, I decided to follow her. As I did so, I heard the muted sound of footsteps and voices. The breeze funneled the sounds into such a vortex that I couldn't tell where they were coming from; then they stopped. I headed to the closest bungalow. I heard a groan, knocked on the door, and entered. I found Lisa on the bed. When I reached down, I felt the knife in her back. I held her wrist; there was no pulse.

It had been foolish of me to touch the knife, but it was too late now, so I hurried back to the house.

When I approached the pool, I heard Mike and headed in his direction.

"Mike."

"What is it, Johnny?"

"Lisa—she's dead. Knifed in the back."

"Oh my God! Where?"

"In one of the bungalows—number three. Find the Clarks, tell them what happened, and call the sheriff. I'm going back to the bungalow to make sure no one contaminates the scene."

Later, when the sheriff arrived at the bungalow, he told me to wait by the pool with the other guests. When I got to the pool, Mike came over, and we sat down at one of the tables.

"Well, Johnny, it looks like the entire sheriff's department is here. That seems odd. I guess they don't get many murders. They've already started taking the guests' fingerprints."

Just as Mike finished, a deputy came over and took my prints.

Eventually the sheriff left the bungalow and came over to the pool to question the guests. He was full of himself and seemed to believe he would find the murderer before the day was over. He wanted everyone to see him in action; I knew the type.

"Who found the body?" he asked.

"I did," I said as I raised my hand.

"I see. And you're, Johnny, right? You're the one who had the altercation with the deceased?"

"No altercation."

"She threw her drink in your face. Not exactly what you would expect between friends, is it?"

"She lost her balance; her drink liked me—it wanted to caress my face." A few of the guests chuckled.

"Oh, a wise guy."

"I assume that since the deceased, Vivian Tuskadaro, was living under an assumed name, there were people after her."

"How'd you know it was Ms. Tuskadaro? No one knew; she's had plastic surgery," the sheriff said in a tone that conveyed immense satisfaction with himself. "You just put a nail in your coffin, Johnny."

"I recognized her voice."

"Her voice," the sheriff echoed before he laughed.

One of the deputies walked over and whispered in his ear.

Mike jumped up and said, "Sheriff, you're making a big mistake, this is—"

"Zip it, mister!" the sheriff shouted. "This is a big-time murder. Lisa—I mean, Ms. Tuskadaro—was in the witness protection program. The commissioner of the NYPD himself told us to keep an eye on her. He's not happy, and he's on his way here by chopper. I think he'll be glad to know we've already apprehended the killer. Don't you think so, Johnny? Your prints are on the murder weapon."

"Well, Sheriff, nothing gets by you."

I heard a chopper in the distance. A few minutes later, the commissioner entered the backyard.

"Hello, commissioner. Good to see you again. Sorry it's under these circumstances," the sheriff said. "But we got the murderer."

I raised my hand. "Apparently I'm the guy."

"This is your murderer?" the commissioner said.

"Yep, he found the body, his prints are on the knife, he knew she was Vivian Tuskadaro, he had an altercation with her, and he's a smart ass," the sheriff said, so very pleased with himself.

"Sheriff, you're an idiot. This is Johnny Duncan, the most decorated officer in NYPD history. Of course he would have had an altercation with her; he spent years trying to incarcerate her father—and did. He's intimately familiar with the voices of everyone in the Tuskadaro family. And yes, he would have touched the knife. He wouldn't have known the knife was in her back until he felt it: he's blind. But you got one thing right, Sheriff: he's a smart ass."

The End

10

The News Not Printed

In 2014 after I had retired as editor of the *Morning Standard*, a longtime college friend, Gary Demarco, called me from his law firm in the state capital. We talked on the phone or got together now and then. Sometimes it would be personal—a get-together of college friends—or it would be business—help with legal aspects of a story.

"Edmund, I've got something you'll want to see—to read. Newspaper articles from the early 1900s with updates written privately by the editor weeks or months later; the movie star's visit to Colvard that wasn't what it seemed, the returning hero from World War I who wasn't what he pretended, and more."

"Where'd you get those?"

"My firm inherited ten boxes from a client. The client had inherited the boxes from his great-uncle. The great-uncle had been a newspaper reporter and editor in Colvard, which was a large town at the time. The boxes contain newspapers and the great-uncle's journals about some of the newspaper's articles. I've read a few of his journals, and you'll find them quite interesting."

"Sure, I'll come down and have a look."

Gary indicated that a reporter from the big city *Times* was doing a story on him, but he'd be able to break away, so I made arrangements to stop by his office the next morning.

When I walked into Gary's outer office, the secretary told me I was expected. "Just go in," she said, so I did.

Gary was at his desk, talking and holding a cigar. He didn't smoke; he used props. Stretched out on the sofa, propped up on one elbow, was a blonde. She was decked out in a long, formal, black dress with a slit that ended the next county over. Two-inch-long earrings dangled from each lobe. She stood when I entered.

"Edmund, great, you're here. Let me introduce you to Tricia Haliwell, the *Times* reporter I was telling you about. And Tricia, this is—"

"Edmund Grandman; it's nice to finally meet you."

"Likewise. I've read your recent piece on Walter Lippmann. Excellent work."

"Perhaps I can do you."

"Thanks, but I'm already well done." I glanced up and down her dress. "But it's nice to see that *Times'* reporters are so well . . . compensated."

"If only. I'm attending a gala for the *Times* later today. The outfit's a rental."

"Too bad. For a second I was considering un-retiring and moving to New York for the pay."

"Come on. We'd gladly take you. I'm sure you could get into anything you wanted," she said with a quick wink.

"Enough already," said Gary. "Tricia, if you'll excuse Edmund and me for an hour or so."

"Sure, I've got plenty of notes to type up. Hope to see you later, Edmund."

I smiled and nodded politely, knowing I would be heading home shortly.

Gary told me to sit next to the stack of boxes at his desk.

"Edmund, the newspapers and journals in these boxes are from random dates between 1900 and 1938. The journals reference the editor's stories in the newspapers, but they were written weeks—sometimes years—after the original stories were published. His journals are titled *The Real Story*. Those real stories have additional information about the published articles. You'll want to read them."

"I'll take them."

Newspaper of May 25, 1917
Daily Mirror Closes—New Presses to Be Installed

The *Daily Mirror*, our crosstown rival, will be closed this week while new Harmon printing presses are being installed. It's been difficult getting parts for the older Waterhouse presses since the Waterhouse company went out of business five years ago. We not only wish our rivals the best, but we're working double shifts to help them install the new presses. Also, during the week, we'll provide our own newspaper free to any subscribers of the *Daily Mirror*. We're on the honor system; we'll take your word.

The Real Story—Newspaper of May 25, 1917
Daily Mirror Closes—New Presses to be Installed

United States postal inspectors, wielding sledgehammers, smashed the presses of the _Daily Mirror_. The United States government had passed the Espionage Act of 1917 during World War I, and the postmaster general had been given censorship authority by the Creel Committee. Action or language deemed unpatriotic was a crime. Newspapers, pacifists, socialists, and labor leaders, among others, were targeted.

The _Daily Mirror's_ crime: it had run a glowing front-page story about Mary Lowell. The fact that Lowell is a Quaker— opposed to both the war and the draft—brought forth the ire of the government. Printing a favorable story, front page no less, about someone with such unpatriotic views was deemed a violation of the Espionage Act. Lowell is, undoubtedly, the most admired person in town. She inherited a textile mill in Massachusetts from her great-uncle when she was 22 and has made benevolent and charitable contributions to the community over the past sixty years while maintaining an extremely frugal lifestyle herself.

Although a smattering of people in town knew the real story, we were threatened if we printed the truth. Our paper would be closed, the owner and employees jailed, and, perhaps, individual employees deported. And, if that weren't enough, private "patriotic" organizations, which the government allowed to act without restraint, would be given the names and addresses of the paper's employees. We knew those vigilante groups could tar and feather, run out of town, or sometimes lynch people labeled as unpatriotic. And the law usually looked the other way. In the few such cases that went to trial, the juries refused to convict the vigilantes, afraid for their own safety. The newspaper's owner took the threat seriously and acquiesced to the government's demands.

I did hear through the grapevine a few months later that Secretary of War Newton Baker, who is thought to have strong pacifist leanings of all things, was appalled by the physical violence committed by postal inspectors. Through his intercession, the administration let it be known that physical violence by the postal authorities was not to be tolerated. However, the full force of the law was still brought to bear, and many folks were sent to prison, and many newspapers closed. Most folks in town who knew the truth freely admitted they would no longer be voting Democratic.

Newspaper of September 1, 1919
Elliott Lemond – War Hero – Running for Mayor

Elliott Lemond, the son of Sam and Sara Lemond (of Lemond Textiles), announced he is running for mayor. The Lemond Textile Company is one of the largest employers in the state. Elliott Lemond is well known for his heroics during World War I. Many will remember that he was hurt during the war and came home in August 1918. Many of his exploits were reported in various newspapers after his return. We hope Elliott Lemond gets what he deserves.

The Real Story - Newspaper of September 1, 1919
Elliott Lemond – War Hero – Running for Mayor

When Elliott Lemond returned home from the war, numerous newspapers—not ours—had story after story of his gallant exploits. The Lemonds kept his *true* exploits out of the papers, but they weren't as successful in restraining the French press. It turns out their son fell from the second-story window of Madame ReRul's in Paris. Elliott was visiting the office—or bedroom, depending on your perspective—of Madame Fontaine when he slipped on his condom wrapper. (Yes, they're illegal in the United States, but not in France.)

Fortunately for him, Elliott missed the wrought iron fence by inches, and his fall was broken by a French woman. For all intents and purposes, Elliott was unhurt. It didn't help matters that it was broad daylight, Elliott was *au natural*, and the woman who broke his fall was the wife of the prefect of Paris (Chief of Police). A short time later, at the local police station, Elliott was pushed down a flight of stairs by the Prefect, which is what caused the broken ribs, broken leg, and twisted ankle that got him sent home. He wasn't pushed because he fell on the Prefect's wife but because Madame Fontaine is, or at least was, the prefect's courtesan. Oh, boy!

Our newspaper's owner, a man of quiet dignity, felt the true story was in poor taste, beneath us, and unworthy of publication. It is interesting to note that soon after Elliott's return home to his wife, his father wasn't shy about disparaging his son. It wasn't long before Mr. Lemond assigned the running of Lemond Textiles to Mrs. Lemond, his daughter-in-law, a graduate of Rensselaer Polytechnic Institute.

———∞∞∞———

Newspaper of July 15, 1927
Local Farmer Captures LA Crime Boss

Ben Johnson, a farmer who lives 10 miles outside of town, was credited with capturing Ringo Torrio, the notorious crime boss formerly of Los Angeles. Torrio is described as so ruthless that Johnson had to use dynamite to subdue him. Torrio was injured during the capture, but authorities have indicated his injuries are not life-threatening.

Unfortunately, part of the H. H. Arnold High School building was damaged during the course of Torrio's capture. Fortunately, the incident occurred on Saturday night when no students were present. Johnson will receive a key to the city and the $1,000 reward for Torrio's capture. Johnson's extended family is well known throughout the county. His great-uncle, Reilly Cornelius, was mayor twenty years ago; his former brother-in-law's uncle is the esteemed evangelist, Hendon Studstill; and his grandmother's sister-in-law, believe it or not, was former sheriff Tootie Crum, who could shoot a pecan out of a squirrel's mouth at a hundred paces, so they say.

The Real Story—Newspaper of July 15, 1927
Local Farmer Captures LA Crime Boss

Ben Johnson did capture Ringo Torrio, but the capture was inadvertent. In truth, Ben was a lucky man. If things had gone as Ben intended, he almost certainly would have been charged with murder. He had no idea who Torrio was, nor any idea that he was in the high school when the dynamite accidentally exploded. In fact, Johnson had planted the dynamite and was planning to set it off on Monday—when school was in session—to protest his property tax bill of $3.23, which he couldn't pay. Property taxes were used exclusively to pay for county educational expenses, teachers' salaries, and the like.

What Ben was really doing was discovered when the sheriff, Earl Hagen, arrived on the scene a short time after the explosion. When he was ten, Earl had been saved from drowning by Ben's brother, so Earl felt he owed the family something and fabricated a story after he recognized Torrio. I discovered the truth several months later when I was visiting Ben. In an inebriated condition, he kept ranting, "I know something you don't know. I know something you don't know."

Being a newspaperman, I naturally encouraged his chatter. The whole story came out. Ben wouldn't have been able to keep the story straight without Earl's notes, which Ben still had. By then I thought it best to let sleeping dogs lie.

Newspaper of January 14, 1938
Bernie Walstein Sentenced to 20 Years in Prison

Bernie Walstein's 20-year-tax-evasion sentence drew gasps from the courtroom crowd, which was not surprising, considering it is the longest prison term for tax-evasion this humble journalist has ever heard of. The facts of the case are odd, but they certainly did not seem to warrant such a sentence.

Walstein did not dispute the fact that he paid no income taxes in 1936 and 1937. However, he claimed he was not attempting to evade paying his taxes. Each year he sent the IRS commissioner a letter indicating that he was unable to determine his tax liability and requested that the commissioner send him a tax bill. Walstein produced copies of the letters; however, the IRS indicated it had no such letters in its files. And besides, the prosecution argued that good intentions are never a justification for lawbreaking.

In spite of the courtroom gasps, the sentence drew little public condemnation. A few brave souls stated that considering the judge was Hoss Sims and that Walstein was of the Hebrew religion, the trial's outcome wasn't a surprise.

Addendum: Several months later, Walstein's appeal was denied.

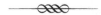

The Real Story—Newspaper of Jan. 14, 1938
Bernie Walstein Sentenced to 20 Years in Prison

I was unsettled about the Walstein verdict after the appeal was denied, so I decided to dig into the matter. Through my contacts with reporters in the nation's capital, I was able to identify two IRS employees who might be willing to browse through their files for me—for a price. It took time, but I was able to arrange a trip to Washington and set up a rendezvous with each employee. The first person was unwilling to do what I asked; the second was willing for a fee—half upfront—which I paid.

Several months later, I received a package of papers from the informant, and I sent him the remaining fee. The package included Walstein's letters, one for each year. They appeared to be the originals. Also included was a letter from another US citizen indicating he was unable to figure his tax liability himself. That exact letter is reproduced below:

March 15, 1936

Honorable Guy T. Helvering
Commissioner of Internal Revenue
Internal Revenue Building
12th St. & Constitution Ave.,
Washington, D. C.

My dear Commissioner Helvering:-

    I am enclosing my income tax return for the cal-
endar year 1935, together with my check for $15,000.
    I am wholly unable to figure out the amount of the
tax for the following reason:
    The first twenty days of January, 1935, were part
of my first term in office and to these twenty days the
income tax rate as of March 1933 apply. To the other
345 days of the year 1935 the income tax rates as they
existed on January, 30, 1935 apply.
    As this is a problem in higher mathematics, may
I ask that the Bureau let me know the amount of the
balance due? The payment of $15,000 doubtless rep-
resents a good deal more than half what the eventual
tax will prove to be.

                  Very sincerely yours,
                  Franklin Delano Roosevelt

I consulted a law firm in the state capital to determine if this new information would warrant a new trial for Walstein. Six weeks later, I received correspondence indicating that an appeal would most likely be successful. Unfortunately, Walstein had died two days before the letter arrived.

Newspaper of June 14, 1938
Joan Crawford Visits Classmate Charles Chub

Our city was most pleased to welcome the actress Joan Crawford during her brief visit. It turns out our town's very own Charles Chub went to high school with Crawford, and she thought it'd be fun to drop in on him unexpectedly. You can see Chub's surprise when Crawford kissed him on the cheek as they posed for photos. Brenda Chub was said to be pleased to meet her husband's longtime friend, now a Hollywood star. Mrs. Chub had just arrived back in town after a two-week stay at the state capital to help her mother convalesce.

The Real Story—Newspaper of June 14, 1938
Joan Crawford Visits Classmate Charles Chub

It wasn't hard to piece together the real story; after all, Brenda is my sister-in-law. The only reason the story was in the paper at all was because Glades Templeton, the paper's human-interest reporter, and Gary Falcon, the paper's photographer, were walking past the Chub house when Crawford walked out the front door.

Crawford didn't go to school with Charles or even know him, at least not before that day. Crawford was passing through town when she ran out of gas in front of the Chub house. When Charles answered the knock at the door, Crawford said, "I need a man." Charles can be quite a charmer if he tries, and it's my understanding that Crawford can be especially friendly. Well, Brenda arrived home an hour later to find her husband and

Crawford in the bedroom having what could best be described as a romp.

I must admit I feel bad for Brenda. The next day she told her best friend, Carla, who lives next door, what really happened. You'd figure Carla, being the preacher's wife, would handle the matter delicately. But all she said was, "Brenda, it was *Joan Crawford* for gosh sakes." That's when Brenda stopped looking for sympathy.

The End

11

Tattoos

As my wife and I strolled through the mall, I nodded in agreement with her comment about tattoos. Yes, it *was* unfortunate that so many people sported tattoos. I couldn't tell her it was because of me, my job, our objective, and the bombings that so many people had them.

At the time, I thought it was the right thing to do; we all did. But it got out of hand and morphed into something far beyond our objective. Now, because of the visual clutter, the intrusion on privacy, and perhaps even the threat to freedom, I agreed with my wife.

In the late 1960s and early 1970s, this country was in turmoil. The crime rate had skyrocketed between 1960 and 1970. From January 1969 to April 1970, there had been more than 4,300 bombings in the United States. Ironically, anti-war radicals were committing most of them. The country seemed to be falling apart. No one remembers that now—bombers running rampant.

The problem wasn't catching the bombers but convicting them. People's ability to recognize faces varies. The general population isn't aware that prosopagnosia—the inability to recognize faces—is prevalent. The acquaintance you walked by in the grocery store wasn't ignoring you, wasn't giving you the cold shoulder; she didn't recognize you. The CIA had determined if a person had a tattoo, they could be identified accurately in court.

I remember the party like it was yesterday. The party where we—our team of CIA operatives—"convinced" our first target to get a tattoo. He was a university's senior class president. His parents were wealthy liberals. The family had been invited to a party a prominent citizen was hosting for the Black Panthers. Bobby, Lisa, and I were charged with *convincing* the class president to get a tattoo. Bobby had a huge Afro, wore jeans, sunglasses, and a T-shirt with "Stop the Fuzz" emblazoned across the front. I wore bell-bottoms, an assortment of beads, a two-day beard, unkempt hair, sandals, and a "Yeah Man, Dig It!" T-shirt. Lisa, with waist-length blond hair, wore hot pants, black boots, and what else but a "Free Love" T-shirt. She was also the one with the fake tattoo. Her tattoo was strategically placed on her chest, half above the waterline and half below. We wanted to get the class president's attention.

After we walked into the penthouse, the butler asked to see our invitation.

"Man," Bobby said with a frown, "we're with the brothers." He nodded at the Panthers.

"I suppose you know the secret—"

"You mean the foot wag?" Bobby extended his right foot toward the butler. The butler did the same until their feet were a foot apart, and then they both wagged. At that we were in.

The butler turned and limped off. Probably had been doing too many foot wags.

We split up and walked around the apartment to get the lay of the land. It was always essential to get an idea of the type of crowd, where the doors and light switches were, who was carrying heat, etc. It was quite a crowd: nerdy types who looked as if they worked at the Federal Reserve, old geezers dressed in colorful robes trying to appear cool (and maybe they were), middle-aged housewives who looked as if they'd rather be anywhere else, and many happy intoxicated partygoers.

When I got back to the living room, I didn't see Bobby or Lisa, so I mingled. In one of the overstuffed comfy chairs, I saw a Panther reading. I was taken aback by his book, so I struck up a conversation.

"Hey, brother, that's quite a read you've got there."

"Can you dig it, man? A first edition, very rare. Found it in the bedroom. One of my favorites."

One of my favorites—surely I misheard him. "*Alice's Adventures in Wonderland*, is one of your favorites?"

"Yeah, man. You need facts, you need curiosity, even though it can be dangerous. Ask Eve or Pandora. Like Alice demonstrates time after time, things may not be what they are said to be."

My eyebrows went up and my head went back.

"You seem surprised, brother, as if reading a great work is unusual for a PhD in English from Harvard."

"No, man, no. I love that book too. A book Winston Churchill recommended for people who wanted to know how governments worked. Just stunned that a brother whose T-shirt is filled with sayings, most which I don't understand, would be reading that. I thought you were a Panther, man."

"I am a Panther. Remember *Alice,* things and people aren't always what they appear to be."

"Power to you, brother, power to you."

I wandered off looking for other interesting people. A young woman sauntered over to me. She put her arms all over me, trying to lie on me as if I were horizontal. She was tooth-some, and her outfit left little—pretty much nothing—to the imagination. She had a heart tattoo above her bellybutton, appeared slightly stoned, and kept caviling.

"The Queen, she stole my dog. Well, not personally, but she had Benji stolen."

"The Queen?"

"Yeah, you know, the Queen of England. MI-5 stole my Benji. I saw Benji sitting on her lap during a TV interview."

I knew she was imagining things. For one, the Queen doesn't do TV interviews.

She said, "Come on, man, show me what's in your pants."

I decided to have a little fun. I couldn't see the harm. She wouldn't remember. I pulled it out, my CIA ID. "This is what's in my pants."

When she saw it, her eyes went wide, she grabbed it, and stuffed it back into my pants. "Damn, don't go showing that around. I'm undercover NYPD."

"Ah . . . look in the mirror; you're certainly not undercover. Nice tattoo by the way. Show me your badge."

"Yeah, right, in this outfit. Oh, if you like body art, you might not mention it to the woman over there," she said. She nodded toward a woman standing by the window. She started to walk away and then turned back to me. "See you later, may-be." She winked.

I looked at the woman the NYPD officer had nodded at. The woman had dirty blonde hair and looked to be in her ear-ly forties. She was dressed nice, not done up or groovy, just dressed like a regular person out for a stroll. Since I still didn't see Bobby or Lisa, I walked over to the woman.

"Hello," I said.

"Hello," the woman replied. She had a bit of an accent,

which I placed as Eastern European.

"I understand you don't like body art, tattoos," I said, perhaps a bit too boldly.

Her eyes narrowed a bit and she chuckled slightly. "No, no I don't. I have an aversion to them. Some of the people I knew during the war were tattooed—numbers across their lower arm."

I knew what she was talking about. The identification method used at Auschwitz and other death camps.

"I'm so sorry. I didn't mean—"

"That's quite all right. You couldn't have known. I am Kazimiera Mika."

"Not Kazimiera Mika from Poland? The picture that—"

"Yes, yes!"

"My gosh. That picture—I have it hanging on the wall in my apartment. I've had it hanging in various rooms of mine since I was fourteen."

"How? You weren't alive when the picture was taken."

"I saw it at fourteen when I was looking through a stack of old *Look* magazines. I hung the picture up to remind me. To remind me of what Edmund Burke said, 'The only thing necessary for the triumph of evil is for good men to do nothing.' Too often we look the other way in the face of evil—thinking it's not that bad, we can handle it, or we don't want to be bothered."

"Few people know that as well as we Poles."

We talked for a few more minutes, and then she left the party. I thought about the picture of her and her sister, Andzia, taken September 14, 1939, by Julien Bryan, an American photojournalist, in Warsaw, Poland, two weeks after Germany had invaded Poland. Kazimiera with an anguished face is kneeling next to her sister, not understanding why her sister, who is lying on the ground, won't speak to her. Then realizing she is dead. Dead by bullets from two Nazi planes that strafed a group of women and girls who were digging up potatoes in a field. That picture was the reason I joined the CIA—to protect the United States and the world from such evil.

In a few minutes Bobby and Lisa were back and we were within sight of the class president. After a few minutes of conversation, Lisa pulled out a joint and lit up. We hoped the combination of Lisa and the joint would attract the class president. Bingo. He stopped chatting with the hostess and walked over.

"What's happening?" the class president said with his nose in the air while his eyes checked out Lisa.

"Cool party, man. You dig it?" asked Bobby.

"You're not bogarting that, are you?" the class president said to Lisa as he nodded at her joint.

"I've got more, brother," Bobby said while pulling a joint out of his pocket. Of course, this one was our special brand and made you groggy fast.

"Where do you guys hang?" the class president asked while tilting his head slightly and rubbing his cheek with the back of his fingers.

"At the village," replied Bobby.

"Oh, yeah. I know people over on the east side," said the class president while nodding.

Lisa giggled. "No, man. The *Cherokee Village* sixty miles up the Hudson. You know, with the real Americans."

"Far out, man," said the class president.

"You think they're groovy too?" said Bobby.

"No, man, far out. They're too far from the city for me to know them," the class president replied.

The hostess had been making the rounds trying to speak

to everyone I suppose. From a distance it looked as if she were enjoying herself since she had a smile on her face. But after she made her way over to us, up-close you could tell the smile was forced. Kind of like she was holding her breath underwater and needed to come up for air.

"I hope you're enjoying yourselves," the hostess said with a drink in one hand.

"The party is out-a-sight," said Bobby.

"I guess so, what with those sunglasses," said the hostess with no sense of irony.

"No, warden chick, Bobby means the party is a gas," I said.

"Please, let's not bring up personal hygiene," said the hostess as she coughed several times, then excused herself.

"What gets you rad, man?" Lisa asked the class president.

"Me, I relax by playing chess, Baby," he said.

"What a coincidence, I relax with boys playing chess," said Lisa.

"Nice tattoo, but I can't tell what it is. Maybe we can rectify that," the class president said with a sly grin while losing his balance.

We had the class president in the physical state we needed. But we noticed the host heading in our direction.

"We can't let the host see the class president in this condition," Bobby said.

"Be cool. I'll take care of it," I replied.

"You having a good time?" the host asked, not noticing the class president yet.

"Yeah, man. Hey, it's cool you've got a first edition of *Alice's Adventures in Wonderland*," I said.

"Yes, that is one of my prized . . . wait . . . that book is in the bedroom."

"Not when I saw it, man."

He turned and scurried away, and we eased the class president out of the penthouse.

We ended up where we wanted, in a hotel room with a tattoo artist the CIA had hired. The next day the class president didn't remember what had happened. For his classmates he made up an elaborate story of the tattoo and why he got it. Two months later he was in prison for bombing the National City Bank, and you can thank the tattoo for putting him there.

With that success, we were authorized to expand the program. We targeted singers, musicians, and other artists. They were always trying to be different, so it was easy to get them interested in tattoos. Our net was wide. We got wildly popular bands and lone singers at local bars to go for tattoos. We were especially successful with movie stars.

The conviction rate for people arrested for bombings skyrocketed, and the bombings dropped off to nothing. I spent eight years in that department. By then, the number of people with tattoos was mushrooming without our help, and I was transferred to another department.

Twenty-five years later, I was transferred back into the tattoo group. What the tattoo program had morphed into blew my mind. CIA front companies owned every company that made tattoo ink. The CIA could track anyone with a tattoo by using the technology in the ink. We could ascertain a person's location at any time. We kept information on millions of people for years. It was kept permanently on some individuals. Had we gone too far? In confronting evil—how far is too far—where do you draw the line? I don't pretend to know. But if you do draw the line, you have to assume you will be tested, you have to be ready to back up *your promise*. Just ask the Poles.

The End

12

The Bag with Bananas and Benjamins

Gwen was standing in the Jiffy Mart paying for her bananas—just bananas. Lightly she laid the bananas in the paper grocery bag and set them on the floor. She opened her purse to put her change away and pulled out the lottery ticket she had bought a few days prior. She checked the numbers once, twice, and then a third time. Gwen hollered, jumped, and then ran outside, continuing her happy hollering and hilarious hoofing. Harvey, her husband, sat in their pickup waiting nearby. Seeing Gwen, he jumped out of the pickup, leaving the door open, ran over, aiming to save her from the wasp or whatever it was that had gotten up her dress or—heaven forbid—her unmentionables.

"What is it? What is it, sweet pea?"

Gwen grabbed his hands, leaned back, and spun Harvey in a circle around her.

"I won the lottery, Harvey, I won the lottery."

"Stop, Gwen. Stop. You're making me dizzier than Tommy Roe."

Little by little Gwen slowed her spinning, not wanting to throw Harvey off balance more than she already had.

"A steak, Harvey. Let's get a steak dinner with all the trimmings."

"Yeah, okay."

They ran to Harvey's truck and headed to the steak house.

A few moments earlier, William Randolph Whitmire, Esq., had driven up to one of the mart's gas pumps. His Rolls Royce had been running on fumes. He was nervous, concerned that he would run out of gas. William had essential tremors, and when he was nervous the shaking worsened. He had to steady his hands to take a drink from his water bottle, which he always had nearby.

As William exited his Rolls, he didn't notice a gust blew one of his business cards off his dash and onto Gwen's seat in the pickup. William proceeded inside to pay for the gas before he started pumping. He didn't see the open grocery bag on the floor with the bananas. As he pulled out his wallet, his hands were still shaking. He didn't believe in credit cards, so he always carried lots of cash—usually hundreds.

William was pulling out a Benjamin when a door slammed in the back of the store. Startled, William flung all the cash out of his wallet. His hands shaking, he picked up the Benjamins from the floor. He was too unsettled to notice five had fallen into the paper bag and lay resting peacefully, cradled with the bananas. With so many Benjamins in his wallet, William was oblivious that a few had vanished. Because a hundred was the smallest bill William had, he gave one to the proprietor and told him to keep the change. He pumped his gas without worrying about getting his hands dirty because he always wore gloves when he was anywhere other than his home—a peculiarity he attributed to Sister Mary Grace. After pumping the gas, he drove to his office in the Whitmire Trust Company building.

Outside the Jiffy Mart, Ellen was sitting in her car, oblivious to Gwen and Harvey and William, talking on the phone with her neighbor, Doris.

"Doris, I'm sure Bertha wasn't a guard at Auschwitz."

"You can't know that, Ellen. She is German. You need to stop bringing her food."

"Doris, I need to go. My dress is caught on the manifold intake. Bye." Her comment was how Ellen replied to Doris's stupidity, by returning the stupidity. Jayson, Ellen's twenty-one-year-old son, who was home from college, sat next to her, bored.

"Jayson, I left my bag in the Jiffy Mart. It's already been paid for. Get it for me, please."

Jayson walked into the mart, saw a bag on the floor at the front checkout, crinkled it closed without peeking inside, and took it. He walked to the car and put the bag on the back seat, while Ellen's actual bag was left sitting on the table across from the register.

When Ellen arrived home, the first trailer in the trailer park, she didn't have to tell Jayson to take the bag to Bertha. Bertha was eighty, retired, and didn't have much income, so every week Ellen brought her some food. Jayson grabbed the bag, headed to Bertha's trailer, and left the bag on the steps as usual.

Bertha lived in a trailer at the end of the street. Technically, she didn't live in the trailer park, but you wouldn't know it—no one did. The trailer park's legal boundary ended at the street's end, and Bertha's trailer sat thirty feet beyond that. Bertha's trailer was on land that was part of a large plot with assorted weeds and such.

Fifteen years earlier, when Bertha was visiting Ellen, Bertha noticed what she assumed was an empty lot at the end of the street. She made arrangements with the power company and the phone company and had her trailer moved to the spot. Bertha was legally a squatter. Because the plot of land was large, none of the prior owners had noticed her trailer. The property had changed hands several times, but none of the prior owners developed the property. The current owner, however, did plan to build on the land, and that was Bertha's current circumstance—they wanted her off *their* property.

Later that day Ellen walked over to visit Bertha. They had met twenty years earlier at the local shoe factory where they both worked. At the time Bertha was hired, she stirred up resentment among some of the workers. Perhaps resentment is too strong a word, but she was treated as a bit of an outcast because of her heavy German accent.

Ellen, who was the union representative at the plant and well-liked, went out of her way to befriend Bertha. People admired Ellen because of her sense of fair play, her balanced approach to things. "You can thank Aristotle for that," Ellen always said. Ellen had been a Peripatetic ever since she had been introduced to Aristotle's works by Ms. Bell, her ninth-grade history teacher.

"Bertha, I've been doing some reading, and I don't think the Peace Organization Over Preferred Egalitarian Doings—POOPED—can kick you off the land. You're a squatter. And since you've lived here for fifteen years, kept the property up and such, you have squatter's rights."

"So, what do I do now?"

"You need a lawyer to handle the matter."

"A lawyer? I can't afford a lawyer."

"I found one for you. The people at legal services gave me

the name of someone who can help you. Here's his card. He only charges ten dollars an hour, and you have an appointment with him this Friday."

"Thanks to some money I've come into," Bertha winked at Ellen, "I should be able to afford that."

Ellen ignored the wink, thinking Bertha had a gnat in her eye.

"Is this lawyer any good?" Bertha asked.

"He should be. He drives a Rolls Royce."

"A Rolls. How can he drive a Rolls charging ten dollars an hour? Something's fishy."

"Fishy is right. He has to perform community service at ten dollars an hour and help the less well-off with legal matters one day a week for a year. Turns out he was eating expensive goldfish out of a restaurant's fish tank. When no one was looking, he'd scoop out a goldfish and swallow it whole. They're not sure how many he ate."

"Why'd he do that?"

"I wouldn't know. Why don't you ask him Friday? Oh, by the way, Doris thinks you might have been a guard at a Nazi concentration camp."

At that, Bertha spit out the Coke that she was drinking.

"What? I wasn't even living in Germany then. And I hated Hitler. He killed Sparkie."

"Sparkie?"

"My dog."

Ellen did a double take.

"Hitler killed your dog?"

"Yes."

"Why would he do that?"

"At the time, 1940, I lived in a small town a hundred kilometers from London. Sparkie had a special talent. He could sniff out Nazi spies."

Ellen looked at Bertha with a frown, skeptical.

"Two new men in town seemed a bit odd. No one knew where they came from, and they were always watching people and taking notes. After all, we did have a plant that made engines for Spitfires on the outskirts of town. Sparkie never barked at anyone except those two men. At some point both men were arrested as Nazi spies. Then one day while I'm at work, a German bomber, the only one over England that day, bombed my house and killed Sparkie. I knew Hitler had given the order. My suspicions were proved several weeks later by Rudolf Hess."

"Rudolf Hess, the number-two guy in Germany after Hitler?"

"Yes, or number three, if you asked Herman Göring. Anyway, Hess flew to England during the war to try to make peace. But first he stopped by to see me. He landed in the field behind my house. I was living in a spare room of Mrs. Martin's next door, since I had no house. Mrs. Martin was not home, thankfully."

"Thankfully."

"Well, he introduced himself and said as a fellow dog lover he wanted to apologize for the death of Sparkie. He said he was sorry about my house too, but at least it could be replaced. He had tried to get Hitler to call off the mission, but he couldn't be dissuaded. Rudolf came inside, and we had a nice cup of tea. Then he had to leave to find the Duke of Hamilton."

"Bertha, are you sure this happened? You've never mentioned this before."

"Yes, Rudolf even told me the code name of the mission, *Red Rover, Red Rover, send Sparkie on over.*"

Ellen burst out laughing. Despite the anguish on Bertha's

face, each time Ellen thought she was done laughing and caught her breath, she started laughing again. Finally, after several minutes of this, she stopped.

"I'm sorry, Bertha, but that seems a bit long for the name of a secret mission."

"I wouldn't know about that."

Ellen had never heard such a fanciful story from Bertha and wondered if age was affecting her memories.

Gwen married Harvey Gaskins when they were both twenty. Now at sixty-five, they were still together and happy. They had met when Harvey pulled over to change Gwen's flat tire on the old Milford Road, which was a dirt road back then. She had told Harvey she was new to town and had no friends and family, which was true, after a fashion. Harvey was an ordinary farm boy who at that time worked at the Farm Supply Emporium. But for the past twenty years, he worked at Freddy's A/C Repair. They married even though Gwen was Catholic and Harvey was Baptist. Harvey was unsophisticated yet Gwen was debonair. Still, they hit it off. Gwen was working at the local sewing plant and still worked there. She never discussed her past during their forty-five years of marriage, and Harvey could not have cared less. They had a natural fit with each other—like a fine pair of gloves. And each night in their prayers, they thanked God for finding the other.

Despite having won the lottery, they were both subdued as they chewed their steak at the restaurant, and they had only a short conversation on the way home.

"Harvey, can we wait to talk about the lottery and perhaps . . . keep it to ourselves for now?"

"Sure, sweet pea." Truth be told, Harvey had been thinking about what vegetables to plant in the garden next year, not the lottery.

On Friday Bertha was ushered into William Whitmire's office after Ms. Johnston, his secretary, had given him some background information on Bertha and the reason for her visit.

"Hello, is this you?" Bertha asked as she handed the card to William.

"Yes, this is my card." William slipped the card into his jacket pocket. When his community service was up, he didn't want his business cards floating around.

"Mr. Whitmire, can I ask you a question?"

"Certainly."

"Why did you eat all those goldfish?"

William was not going to spend half an hour explaining to Bertha about the nun at Saint Bartholomew's orphanage. He had been left on the steps when he was three days old and lived there until he was eighteen. Sister Mary Grace would paddle his hands at the slightest infraction. She made him wait alone in her office before his punishment, giving him time to agonize. What Sister Mary Grace seemed to love above all else were both her goldfish and her large office, which conveyed preeminence. A large fish tank was on the opposite wall from the long wooden bench where children would wait. On occasion, while waiting in her office, William would glide over to the fish tank and swallow one or two of her cherished goldfish whole—a crime leaving no telltale evidence.

The current goldfish episode was some kind of flashback.

The restaurant hadn't wanted to prosecute William, considering he was one of its best customers. Unfortunately, the matter had been reported to the police and picked up by the local paper. Since it was election time and the district attorney couldn't be seen letting a wealthy man off, it was agreed that he would serve time doing community service.

William's face turned slightly red. "They're an aphrodisiac," he replied.

"Poisonous and you'd eat'em? Why didn't you die?"

William squinted, assessing Bertha's question—well, not the question so much as her frame of mind.

"If you start out small, just swallowing the tail, your body can adjust to the poison. Are you sure you're from Germany?"

"Yes, why?"

"Never mind. Did you pay property taxes on the land where you're living?"

"No, never did."

"Hum . . . that might be a problem."

"I didn't have to since I was a HELPME volunteer."

"HELPME?"

"Help the Elderly Limit Property Money Egress. You see, if you are over sixty-five and work at the property tax office for eight hours every month, you are exempt from property taxes. And you didn't have to work eight hours straight. You could split it and work two four-hour shifts. Or if you had an emergency—"

"Yes, yes, I see. That will be very helpful. Even though I'm a patent lawyer, I should be able to help you with this."

"Thank you, Mr. Whitmire. And I'm glad you're a patient lawyer. Most people aren't patient with me anymore."

"Thank you, Bertha. I'll call you when I have the hearing arranged."

"Oh, I'm sorry you're having trouble with your hearing. I hope you can get it arranged."

At that William escorted Bertha out of his office. He sat at his desk for a few minutes, reflecting. Here he was, forty-five, wealthy, and with a job he enjoyed. Many lawyers found patent work dreary, but not him. He was wealthy because he and James Styles had bought land on the outskirts of the city when they were twenty-five. As luck would have it, five years later, the city decided to build an airport close to their plot, and the price of the land skyrocketed. They sold their plot. Two requirements of the sale were that William's name go on the building to be built and he be allowed an office rent-free for life. James, meanwhile, had moved to the south of France.

"Mr. Whitmire, your next appointment is here. A Mrs. Gwen Gaskins," Ms. Johnston said over the intercom. Gwen had not been willing to share with Ms. Johnston the reason for her appointment. That, in itself, didn't seem unusual.

"Okay, send her in."

William met Gwen at the door as she entered, extending his gloved hand for a shake.

"How do you do, Mrs. Gaskins? Please have a seat and tell me what I can do for you."

"Everything we discuss is confidential—is that right?" Gwen said as she adjusted her dress and looked directly at William.

"Of course, unless you tell me about a crime that's going to occur. Especially a crime where others will be hurt."

"Then we're fine. I won the lottery, the huge jackpot from a few days ago."

"I see. Congratulations."

"The congratulations are premature, I believe. Is my understanding correct that in this state a winner's identity cannot be kept secret?"

"Yes, the government feels that anonymity would allow the government to collude with the lottery and manipulate the winners."

"Can a corporation or trust be set up to hide the winner's identity?"

"No, the winnings can only be claimed by an individual. And Mrs. Gaskins, that individual has to be the person who bought the ticket. The rate of breaking and entering for lottery tickets skyrocketed after the lottery started, and this requirement put an end to that. If you recall, when you purchased the ticket, you had to put your thumb on a scanner. When you claim the winnings, they check your thumbprint against the thumbprint made during the purchase. May I ask, is having your picture and name made public a problem?"

"Yes, it is. When I was young, I was naïve and tempestuous. I did things I shouldn't have, one thing in particular. My life has turned out fine though. I have the best husband I can imagine and a wonderful life. We both will be retiring next month, and I won't risk my husband finding out about my past." Gwen's speech was halting at moments due to its serious nature and Gwen's quest for the right words. "Exposing my identity could potentially harm others also. For the past twenty-five years, I've volunteered at Saint Bartholomew's orphanage at the suggestion of a priest during my confession for penance—for what I did."

William strode over to his water pitcher and poured a glass. He gave the glass to Gwen, who took a few sips and set the glass on the edge of his desk.

"I see. That leaves you only one option."

"Yes, yes it does—destroy the ticket. I do appreciate your help. What do I owe you?"

"Nothing."

"But—"

"I'm not allowed to bill if my service takes less than an hour." A lie.

"One more question. Won't the lottery track me down since my fingerprint is linked to the winning number?"

"No, they can use the fingerprint only to confirm a winner, nothing more."

After Gwen left, William walked to the window, looking at nothing in particular while the fingernail of his right thumb went back and forth over his chin. He took out his handkerchief, went to his desk, wrapped the cloth around Gwen's glass, and sat.

"Ms. Johnston, get me Danny Wilkens on the phone."

A few minutes later Ms. Johnston buzzed William.

"Mr. Wilkens is on line one, sir."

"Thanks, Ms. Johnston. And hold my calls for the rest of the day." He punched the phone button and said, "Danny, how are you doing? I don't think I've seen you since the charity tennis tournament at the club a few months ago."

"Doing fine, William. That's probably right. I eat supper at the club on Wednesdays and Saturdays after golf. I guess our paths just haven't crossed."

"I guess not. I'll occasionally have supper there on Fridays but haven't done much else lately. We'll have to pick a time and play a game or two of chess."

"Great. What can I do for you in the meantime?"

"I'd like you to run a DNA sample for me."

"Sure, is it for court?"

"No, it's a personal matter. I'll give you my DNA to compare it with."

"Okay. But since it's personal, I'll have to charge you for

it."

They both laughed, as if that would be a problem.

Thirty minutes later, William was in Danny's lab, a large room filled with all sorts of scientific equipment. On William's way to Danny's desk at the back of the room, he stopped, pulled Mrs. Gaskins's glass out of his pocket, and set it on one of the lab tables.

Danny was a short, thin man with the face of Joel McCrea and blond hair.

"Danny, I'd like you to compare the DNA on that," William said as he pointed to where he had sat the glass on the distant table, "with my DNA. Is it possible to get DNA from fingerprints?"

"As long as they're not more than a week old."

"Great."

Danny handed William a swab.

"Here, swab this inside your mouth. You think it might be one of your parents?"

"Maybe my mother. I don't like to get my hopes up, but I have a strong feeling this time."

"I know in the past you've debated about whether finding your parents is the right thing to do. And this is what, the third time in the past ten years that I've done this for you?"

"Yes, but finding them and contacting them are two different things. And now I feel that I'd at least like to know. Whether or not I contact them will be the dilemma."

"I'll call you when I have the results," Danny said. He put the swab into a plastic bag.

The following Tuesday William, Bertha, and POOPED

were in court.

"Your Honor, I turned in voluminous data to the court a week ago that proves beyond any doubt that Ms. Buggendorf is a squatter and therefore entitled to stay on the land currently occupied by her trailer at the boundaries indicated on exhibit one."

"I have reviewed the information, Mr. Whitmire. I agree that Ms. Buggendorf is entitled to stay on the land. However, she will have to pay for the property at its value as of fifteen years ago. I trust you and POOPED can work out an equitable arrangement."

"Thank you, Your Honor."

"Mr. Whitmire?"

"Yes, Bertha."

"Do I need to stop by a flower shop and get an equitable arrangement, although I don't know what kind of flower an equitable is?"

William smiled. "No, Bertha, I'll take care of it."

The phone rang in William's office. "William, Danny here. One of the two DNA samples on what you gave me was a 99 percent match to yours." One of the two? Of course, Ms. Johnston, his secretary, would have touched the glass, but she was only twenty-eight and could therefore be eliminated as a maternal possibility. But what about her being a sister?

"A sibling wouldn't be a 99 percent match, would it?"

"No, not unless they were an identical twin. It has to be a parent."

"Okay, thanks, Danny. That's great news."

William hung up. Now that he knew Gwen was his mother,

he needed to decide whether he should let her know.

Four weeks had passed since Gwen discovered she had won the lottery, and she and Harvey had not discussed it since that first day. Harvey had hardly thought about it—not at all really, but Gwen thought about it every day. Five years earlier, Harvey and Gwen had reviewed their retirement finances and knew they could safely retire at sixty-five. Harvey would receive a monthly pension of $450 from Freddy's A/C Repair, and Gwen would get $650 from the sewing plant. They would both start Social Security. They had no debts and estimated their retirement income would be double what they needed to live on. Harvey's 401(k) plan had $80,000 in it, which they would use for emergencies, if necessary. Gwen had a 401(k) also, but they had no idea how much was in it. At the time she was hired, she had read an interview with Jack Bogle, the founder of Vanguard, in the paper. Gwen signed up, contributing 10 percent of her pay to a Vanguard 500 Index fund. Jack had said if people put 10 percent of their pay into a low-cost index fund and did not look at their statement until they retired, they would be pleasantly surprised. Gwen had done just that, tearing up each quarterly statement she received.

They had finished washing and drying the dishes, when Gwen decided she couldn't wait any longer to talk to Harvey about the lottery—and her past.

"Harvey, I have something I need to talk to you about."

"Okay, sweet pea."

"It's about the lottery."

"Oh, that. To tell the truth, I haven't thought about it."

"You haven't? Not about what you could do or what we

could buy?"

Harvey shrugged as if it required no more thought than whether he should have another glass of iced tea. "Nope. What more do we need, sweet pea?"

"My gosh, Harvey. I . . . I need to tell you about something. Something that happened before we met. Something I did."

"You don't need to tell me anything, sweet pea."

"I must, Harvey. I must tell you."

"Sweet pea, I know about you and what you did before we met."

"Harvey, please, you couldn't know. I have to tell you."

"So, what are you going to tell me, sweet pea? That you were brought here forty-five years ago by federal marshals, given a thousand dollars, and a handshake? That your death had been faked by the marshals after you testified against Charles Manson? That you turned your back on your loving family and on the full scholarship to Stanford University to join the Charles Manson family? And the one time you went out with them, you called 9-1-1 from an upstairs bedroom to get help for the people they attacked?"

Gwen hugged Harvey, crying. "You knew? You knew? How?"

"The marshal service gets newspapers from the cities where witnesses are relocated. One of the federal marshals read about our upcoming wedding in the paper. He came to see me a week before the wedding and told me."

"And you still wanted to marry me?" Gwen choked out over her crying.

"Yes, sweet pea. I never had any doubt that you would be the best wife a man could have. People make mistakes."

Gwen kept crying while hugging Harvey.

"Can we take care of the ticket now, Harvey? I've got a

homemade apple pie we can have to celebrate its demise."

"Sure."

The apple pie was placed on the table with one scoop of iced cream and a lit candle in the middle. Harvey and Gwen sat side by side at the table. Gwen held a corner of the lottery ticket over the flame. The flame danced along the ticket that slowly burned up, destroying it along with the sins of the past from Gwen's mind. At last.

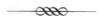

"Hi, William, Danny here. I was curious if you have done anything about the DNA match?"

"No, I haven't. I keep wondering if it was the right thing to do, to give Gwen the glass so I could get her DNA without her consent."

"Glass? What glass?"

"The glass you ran the DNA sample on."

"William, I didn't run the DNA from the glass. I thought that was your glass. You always have a bottle or glass of water with you."

"What? Then where did you get the DNA?"

"From your business card. You left your business card on the lab counter next to the glass."

"Good gosh." William realized the card must have come out of this pocket when he pulled out the glass. The card that Bertha had given him. But it couldn't be Bertha's DNA that matched his. She hadn't moved to the US until 1980. Someone else must have touched the business card.

"I am so sorry, William. Does this mess things up?"

"No, no, not since I haven't done anything. I don't know who the match is, but I can find out. And please, don't apologize.

If I hadn't pulled out my card by accident, you wouldn't have gotten a match."

The next day William stopped by Bertha's trailer to give her the deed to her land.

"Thank you, Mr. Whitmire, but this has *Paid In Full* stamped on it. Wasn't I going to have to work out a payment plan?"

A slight grin settled on William's face, a knowing grin.

"Bertha, the judge called me to explain there was an exception. No payment was needed since the statute of limitations was up."

"Can't imagine what a statue has to do with it. So, it's mine free and clear?"

"Yes."

"Thank you, Mr. Whitmire," Bertha said with the biggest grin William had seen in a while.

"You are welcome, Bertha. I do have one question though. Who gave you my card?"

"Ellen. She lives at the end of the street. The last trailer on the left. It's yellow."

"Thank you and good day."

William drove down to the yellow trailer, went to the door, and rang the doorbell. The door squeaked as it opened.

"Yes, may I help you?" Ellen asked.

"Excuse me, are you Ellen? Bertha said you gave her my card."

Ellen leaned to the right and looked around William to the street.

"Oh, you're the lawyer with the Rolls who helped Bertha

and who thinks goldfish are tasty. Quite an inclination you've got there," Ellen said as she slapped William on the shoulder.

"It's your fault I like goldfish."

"Excuse me."

"It's because of you I eat goldfish."

"What on earth are you talking about?" Ellen asked with a frown.

"If I may come in, I'll explain it—Mother."

The End

13

Extortion or Blackmail

I expected it to be a normal day, most days are. I was wrong. Usually, you don't wonder throughout the day why people call it extortion, when you think perhaps it is blackmail. It seemed to me that one involved violence or the threat of violence, and the other did not.

Gerald Trulock and I, Troy Nash, were partners in the advertising agency Nash & Trulock in a city of just over 450,000. Gerald handled the more conservative clients. I handled the clients who were in a hurry and more interested in pushing the boundaries. I could hook clients at a party or lunch and have them reeled in by day's end.

My routine on that Tuesday started as normal: shower, shave, dress, and on to work. But first, I always stopped for breakfast. It could be the local coffee shop for a decaf and croissant or the King Hotel for unsweetened iced tea and caviar on crackers.

It was the coffee shop that day. The *woman* walked up to my table. She was well dressed in expensive clothes and high heels. She looked to be five or so years younger than me, maybe thirty-five. Her hair was thick, brunette, curled, and flowed a foot below her shoulders. Her makeup was subtle. She looked confident and smart.

"May I?" she asked, glancing at the empty chair across from me.

"Certainly." I was always open to opportunities, and most people knew I was in the ad business.

"You know why I'm here?" she asked.

"Not completely."

"I have the message, sort of. I need your help with it."

"Message. And I can help you with that?"

"Indeed."

"Perhaps you can show me the message, and I'll see."

"It's not that easy."

"Oh?"

"The message is only twenty-five words. I have all of them, but they're not in order. You will need to help me find them and determine their order."

"Find them? I thought you said you had all the words."

"I do. But the words have been tattooed on my body, many in places I cannot see."

"How is it you decided to contact me?"

"Your socks."

"Of course, the socks." I had no clue as to what she meant by that, and I couldn't deftly investigate my socks at that moment.

"Meet me at the King Hotel at noon. Room 214—it's reserved—and you can examine me there. Then we'll have lunch. I know I'm usually hungry after."

After *what* exactly, she didn't say.

"What do I call you?" I wanted her name, though I doubted it would be her real name; still, it was worth a try.

"Darling. And that's what I'll call you too. After all, you are a darling, from what I gather."

With that, she stood and sashayed away without looking back. Marlene Dietrich couldn't have done it better. The first thing that came to my mind was extortion. The police had recently warned many well-to-do local citizens of an extortion racket that was targeting prominent businesspeople. But due to the ongoing investigation, the police offered few details about how the gang operated. The one thing the police did tell us was that a monthly payment was required, and that it was routed through a bank in Liechtenstein. Given the department's limited resources, the police said we should hire a private detective if we suspected anything. I decided to do just that. One of our employees had needed a private eye not long ago and had highly recommended McCallum & McCallum—two sisters who had been in the business for fifteen years. Occasionally I read an article about their firm in the local paper.

I stared down at my socks. They were mismatched—slightly. I hadn't noticed. I headed over to McCallum & McCallum. I told the receptionist I didn't have an appointment. She said that wouldn't be a problem, but I'd have to wait. I sat on the black leather sofa that ran along the wall and picked up a newspaper. I heard the outer door open, and someone entered. Then I heard the receptionist. say, "Good morning, Ms. McCallum."

I peeked over the newspaper then thrust it back up to hide my face when I recognized the woman. It was Darling.

"Is Sierra in?" Darling asked.

"Yes, she's with a client. We do have someone new waiting." I imagined the receptionist was pointing at me.

"Okay, I'll talk to him. Give me a minute, and I'll buzz you." I heard a door open and close. I got up and meandered closer and closer to the front door. When the receptionist's phone rang, I absquatulated to my car.

Driving to the office, I figured Darling was the extortionist, although the setup—meeting a woman who intended to disrobe in a hotel room—didn't exactly feel like extortion.

When I reached the office, Gerald seemed eager to see me.

"Troy, I'm glad you're here. I was going to call you."

"What's up?"

"Jason Gamble of Gamble Cookies is in town, and he wants to talk business. Even though they are headquartered in Chicago, you know I've been after their business for years."

"I thought Samuel Gamble ran the company?"

"Not anymore. Jason is his grandson, and he's displeased with their current ad agency. He wants fresh ideas. From what I've gleaned, he's very avant-garde."

"This is a great opportunity. If we could land him, he would be our biggest client."

"You mean if *you* land him. He wants to meet with you alone at the King Hotel at noon."

"The King . . . today?"

"Yes. Something wrong?"

"No, no . . . not at all. I'll meet with him."

Gerald had already put his Gamble file on my desk. I was going to pull up the Gamble website for a quick, general overview. But first I wanted to see what I could find out about Darling, so I pulled up the McCallum & McCallum website. There were photographs of Darling, real name Ilene McCallum, and her sister Sierra. I wondered if both were involved in the extortion scheme. That would be brilliant. After all, through their legitimate business they could learn many facts that would help them determine their targets. And they would know how the police worked and what tools they used.

They might even have informants in the police department.

I had no choice but to show up at the King to meet Gamble, and there wasn't enough time to alert the police beforehand. At 11:47 a.m. I was approaching the desk at the King Hotel when I heard someone call out.

"Troy, Troy Nash!" I turned and recognized Gamble; I had seen his picture. He took hold of my hand and gave it a firm shake. "Pleased to meet you. Call me Jason. I've already reserved a table. I understand the King has the best food in town."

"Yes, they do. I eat breakfast here on occasion."

"Wonderful. Let's have a seat."

We talked for a few minutes before we ordered. Jason said that even where he lived, Chicago, he had heard of me. He wanted new ideas—something fresh.

The server arrived to take our order. He spoke with an accent, and Jason unabashedly asked where he was from. "Nigeria," the waiter replied matter-of-factly. Jason ordered his food in a language I didn't understand. The astonished server broadly grinned, no doubt astonished to hear his own language. The server finished taking our order and headed to the kitchen with the grin still plastered to his face.

"What language was that?" I asked.

"Hausa. Most people in Nigeria speak it."

"How in the world did you learn it?"

"My parents were great believers in learning languages. My siblings and I started learning languages when we were three. The challenge was to learn one language each from South America, Europe, Africa, and Asia."

"That's impressive. I understand if you learn another language by the age of seven, you can speak it like a native. Kudos to your parents."

"I am grateful now, to be sure."

As I glanced toward the restaurant's entrance, I saw Ilene McCallum heading toward us, and she called out. "Darling, I didn't know you were going to be here."

"Yes, unexpected business meeting," I said as I stood.

"How do you do?" Darling offered her hand to Jason, who stood too. "I'm Ilene Nash, Troy's wife."

What! Oh, God! Somehow I maintained my composure even as Ilene put her arm around my waist and kissed me on the lips.

"Please, Mrs. Nash, join us. I'm Jason Gamble."

"Thank you. I will. And it's Ilene, please."

"Certainly."

"Darling," I said as casually as I could, "what are you doing here?"

"My sister, Sierra, has come to town unexpectedly. I spent the morning with her."

"Ilene, I'm glad to meet Troy's wife. I'm considering giving him the ad account for Gamble Cookies."

"That is grand. Our daughter loves your cookies. Delights are her favorite."

I almost choked on my sip of water.

"I've done some research on Troy, and I wasn't aware you had a daughter."

"That surprises a lot of people," I said, trying not to show surprise myself.

"If you don't mind, Darling, I have a few suggestions for Jason," Ilene said.

"I don't know that you should bother Jason with—"

Jason interrupted. "Why, Troy, I don't mind at all. I'm curious. Go ahead, Ilene."

"The boldest idea would be to convince a TV network to create a cartoon based on the cookies."

"And you could do that?"

"It's extremely difficult, but Troy and I know a few TV producers. It's a long shot and would involve up-front money. Also, you're limiting your market by only going after the youngsters. You're missing other demographics. The key is to test various demographics instead of going all in on one; cast many small nets and see what jumps in."

"What other demographics, Ilene?"

"Well, think of places where people are sitting down eating snacks, like nursing homes. You could sell cookies infused with vitamins—vitamin D, for example—that older people need. And what about sports fans? Get them off the chips. The tailgating football crowd might like cookies with names like Quarterback or Receiver, each one in a different flavor, and maybe even in a different shape."

"You think there are possibilities there?" Jason asked.

"Certainly. Remember, most ideas don't pan out, so don't get frustrated."

"I've been thinking about a video game based on the cookies," Jason said. "What's your opinion on that, Ilene?"

Jason didn't even glance at me.

"Don't do it. Unless the graphics are top-notch, the game will appear second-rate, and that feeling would carry over to the cookies. Outstanding video games take years to develop, and the people playing them are already your customers.

"Excellent insights, Ilene." Jason looked over to me and said, "Troy, I guess I have discovered your secret: Ilene is remarkable."

"She's something else all right."

Ilene grinned at me. I realized she was no ordinary extortionist. I had never met anyone so quick on her feet. If she weren't a criminal, I would have wanted to hire her.

At that moment both Jason and Ilene looked up to

something behind me. Ilene smiled and quickly stood up.

"Tess! Tess Hamilton! Imagine running into you here. How are you?"

Tess is my wife's first name, and Hamilton is her maiden name. By the time I stood and turned around, Ilene was hugging my wife. Tess looked startled—I knew the feeling.

"Tess, do you know my husband, Troy?"

"Why . . . yes, yes I do. But maybe I don't know him as well as I thought."

I reached out to shake Tess's hand; I almost had to grab it. "Hello. This is Jason Gamble of Gamble Cookies," I said, and I nodded at Jason. "He may become a new client, an important client."

"So discretion is the better part of valor?"

"Exactly, Darl . . . Te . . . Ms. Hamilton."

"Listen, Tess," Ilene said. "I have to take my sister to the airport in a few minutes. Can I drop you off on the way? I'll be going right by your house."

"Yes, that would be delightful. Maybe we can catch up. I'd love to hear the latest on your and Troy's affairs."

"If you gentlemen will excuse us then, Tess and I will be on our way." Ilene kissed me on the lips and strolled off with Tess, who turned and gave me a stern look as they left. As I sat down I scanned the room for Rod Serling of *Twilight Zone* fame.

"Troy, I'll give your agency a try. While we eat I'll go over what I'd like in the contract. I fly home this afternoon, but if you'll overnight the contract to me later this week, maybe I can fly back next week to sign the deal. How does that sound?"

"Sounds perfect."

After lunch and good-byes with Jason, I called Tess to be sure she got home okay. Doris, our maidservant, answered and called Tess to the phone. Tess was curt. I told her I'd be home soon and explain everything. Explain everything, who was I kidding. The truth would have to do. My office was on the way home, so I made a quick stop.

Ilene certainly was artful. It would take someone smooth to run an extortion or blackmail racket, and Ilene seemed more than up to the task. At least she hadn't fouled up the deal with Gamble Cookies.

Gerald was pleased when I told him the outcome of my meeting with Jason. I didn't go into detail. I was in my office hurriedly finishing up when my secretary buzzed.

"Mr. Nash, there's a woman here who insists on seeing you."

"Who is it?"

"Sierra McCallum."

I figured the more I could learn before going to the police, the better.

"Send her in."

She approached and placed two pictures on my desk. One was of Ilene and me at the coffee shop. The other picture showed Ilene kissing me at the restaurant.

"How do you do, Ms. McCallum? Or should I call you Sierra, considering you're one of the family, after a fashion?"

Sierra ignored what I thought was a clever comment. "Kissing someone who is not your wife could hurt the business, couldn't it? And your wife might not be too pleased either. But two-hundred thousand dollars would make these pictures disappear forever."

"Ms. McCallum, extortion is a nasty business. Leave, or I'll call the police." I picked up the phone.

"Extortion? Why do you think . . . oh, of course, the police warning. If you call the police, I promise you'll regret it.

A discussion with your wife and what transpired between her and Ilene will be telling. I'll call you tomorrow with instructions for the money transfer." With that, Sierra turned and marched out the door.

I wanted to call the police, but I didn't want to spend all afternoon at the police station before talking with Tess, so I put the phone down and left for home.

When I walked into the den, Tess was lying on the sofa, propped up on one elbow reading *It's a Woman's World,* an excellent magazine. The articles on current events are second to none. They hire reporters, not journalists. Reporters report the facts and let you decide, not using adjectives and adverbs to slant the article one way or the other. Journalists, I have noticed, are more concerned with their own popularity.

I always read the article on the trailblazing woman of the month. Last month it was on Clara Brett Martin, the first woman in the British Empire to become a lawyer. Of course, I rarely read the articles on clothes, makeup, shoes, computer coding, engine mechanics, or the math problem of the month.

Tess hadn't said a word. Finally, she sat up.

"Quite the ladies' man, aren't we, darling?"

"Good heavens, Tess. Ilene and her sister are running the extortion racket the police warned us about; although, it seems to me more a matter of blackmail. Her sister, Sierra, stopped by my office today and demanded two-hundred thousand dollars. I'm glad you're okay. What in the world did you and Ilene talk about?"

"You, mostly, comparing notes."

"Please. That would have been a short conversation; she doesn't know me."

"She knows more than you think—a lot more. She did say your kisses weren't passionate, by the way."

"Good grief. Those weren't kisses; those were put-ons."

"I have a surprise for you. Seeing how you like women so much, I bought Doris a new outfit."

Uh-oh. I looked questioningly at Tess. She had a slight smile, her face glimmering with a mischievous expression.

Tess picked up a small bell and rang it. Doris backed into the den wearing her new maidservant's uniform while bent over the cart to keep the drinks from spilling. My eyes went straight to her legs as her new skirt was extremely short.

I turned to Tess with a frown, the corner of my mouth pulled to one side.

Doris leaned over me with my drink.

"Sir," she said.

I turned and stared at the drink, then up at her. I froze for a second. "Bloody hell, Tess! What's this?"

Tess burst out laughing. I had assumed it was Doris leaning over me with the drink, but it was Ilene who was wearing the maidservant's uniform. And Sierra slipped into the den laughing with the other two.

"What the heck?"

Amid the laughing, Tess said, "Ilene, Sierra, and I know each other from college. We're sorority sisters, and the sorority is having an alumni contest: ten thousand dollars to the woman who can pull off the best prank on her husband." Ilene plopped onto my lap and kissed me for the third time as a flash went off. But this time I kissed her back. *Not passionate enough? We'll see.* Ilene didn't seem to mind, although that bit of frivolity cost me my percentage of the prize money. Serves me right, I admit. That wasn't to be the last prank these sagacious women would pull on me over the years.

The End

14

The Judge, the Trial, the Kidnapping

Moose was standing nonchalantly at the newsstand across the street from the coffee shop pretending to read his paper. After a few minutes he walked to the corner, where Roy was waiting.

"The Judge and her husband are still eating lunch, just like they've been doing every day for the past two weeks," Moose said.

"Great. I'll get the van. You know what to do," Roy said.

"Okay." Moose headed back to the newsstand and continued watching their quarry.

Soon after, the Judge left the coffee shop, but Dashiell stayed to finish his meal. Once the Judge was out of sight, Moose waved to Roy, who pulled a nondescript white van up to the curb, stopping in front of an alley two stores down from the coffee shop. Moose crossed the street and slipped into the alley. He took a bottle and a handkerchief from his coat pocket and poured the liquid onto his handkerchief.

When Dashiell left the coffee shop and walked past the

van, Moose jumped out and grabbed him. He held the hand-kerchief soaked with chloroform over the man's nose and mouth. Roy got out and helped corral Dashiell into the van. He was out within seconds.

"Dennis is as good as free now that we've got the Judge's husband," Roy said.

"Yeah," Moose replied.

Two hours later, the van pulled up to an abandoned cabin off the beaten path. The husband could shout as much as he wanted; no one would hear.

After lunch the Judge entered the courthouse and walked into her chambers. She had enjoyed lunch at the coffee shop and was glad they could make time for each other. With their schedules, it was unusual that they could have lunch together every day for two weeks straight. She put on her robe and pre-pared to continue with the trial of Dennis Griner, who was charged with bank robbery. Because Dennis had a gun during the robbery—even though he hadn't brandished it—he could get sentenced for up to twenty-five years.

At home that evening, the Judge was going through her mail and found an envelope with Judge written on it. When she opened the envelope, she found a message of crudely cut magazine letters pasted on an otherwise blank paper:

We kidnapped your husband from the coffee shop. Free Dennis Griner. No Police.

The Judge's husband wasn't home; he wasn't supposed to be. He was going out of town after lunch today, so the Judge wasn't concerned. Besides, she was always getting kooky notes and prank phone calls.

Later that evening the Judge's phone rang. "Hello?"

"You got the message? We don't want no trouble, or else. You free Dennis Griner tomorrow."

"How am I supposed to do that?" said the Judge with an air of indifference.

"What?" said Moose not so much to the Judge as to himself.

"How am I supposed to free him?" the Judge asked nonchalantly.

"What do ya mean? You're a judge."

"So you've been to law school? You can tell me my business?"

"Well . . . no, but movies, TV shows, always show . . . and Roy said—"

"Roy said, now Roy is telling me my business. Listen, we have rules and procedures to follow. We can't just magically make things happen. You've been watching too much TV. And how do I know he's still alive?"

"What?" Again Moose was at a loss as to what was happening.

"How do I know he's even still alive?" At that, the Judge hung up the phone.

Moose pulled the phone away from his face and stared at it, wondering how a simple phone call could have gone wrong. He walked to the nearby dumpster and tossed the burner phone. Roy said they had to buy a burner phone every time they called the Judge. Moose knew Roy would be mad when he got back to the cabin.

The Judge sat down for a minute, considering her options. She'd have to tell the chief of police, but not yet. The Judge believed that the best way to handle unexpected surprises by bad people was to surprise them back. And the best way to do that was to do something *they* weren't expecting. Time after time, she had gotten the upper hand that way. She took a hot bubble bath, went to bed, and slept like a baby, which wasn't unusual for her. The Judge was considered valiant by everyone who knew her.

As Moose was driving back to the cabin, he wondered how to explain the phone call to Roy. The more he thought about it, the more confused he got about exactly how it went wrong. If he couldn't explain it to himself, How could he explain it to Roy? And Roy could be mean. At just that moment, the song "You Don't Mess Around With Jim" came on the oldies station; Moose turned it off. He hated that song. It reminded him that Slim was a sissy compared to Roy.

When Moose came into the cabin, Roy was sitting at the table reading the *Sporting News*. The husband was tied up in the back room.

"Things go all right?" Roy asked.

"I . . . don't think . . . I mean, I don't know."

Roy was propped up on his elbows, his chin resting on his hands. He squinted at Moose while his left thumb moved slowly back and forth over the scar on his left cheek. He looked hard at Moose, his eyes demanding an explanation.

"She got me confused right off. She asked me stuff we hadn't talked about. And she hung up."

Roy sat silently. He rubbed his eyes with the palms of his hands, thinking. "What's supposed to happen next?"

"I don't know, Roy. Like I said, she hung up."

"Moose, this was the easiest part in the plan, and you bungled it," Roy said while shaking his head.

Moose sat down, afraid to say any more.

It was times like this that Roy wouldn't hurt Moose—times he felt sorry for him, sorry for his intellect, or rather lack of it. "Tomorrow night I'll go into town and call her. Let's check on the husband and go to bed."

The next day was a typical workday for the Judge. She thought about the kidnapping now and then, especially during lunch when she ate alone in the coffee shop. She was concerned about Dashiell but felt he wasn't in any danger. At least not yet. He taught at a law school that was only two blocks from the coffee shop, and lunches were one of the few times they had together with no interruptions, to discuss the law, which they both loved. Of course, sometimes he'd get too flirty in public. He'd remind her that no one could kiss like she could, hinting. The Judge parried his amorousness.

When the Judge returned to her chambers, she called the police commissioner, Iris Evans, and asked her to come to her chambers the next day at six p.m. on a matter of importance. Iris was out of town but would be back in time to meet with the Judge. The Judge expected Dennis Griner's trial to wrap up the next day, and she'd announce her verdict the following day.

Roy attended the trial most days. He had bought a new suit and got gussied up on those days. After all, he didn't want to look like a bank robber's accomplice. Moose and Roy had helped with the robbery. They even had the loot. They had been in the getaway car, on the corner of Fifth and Elm with the windows down, waiting for Dennis to come running and jump in. When Dennis rounded the corner, he had thrown the duffel bag into the car but kept running. The police were too close, and Dennis knew it. After the police ran by in pursuit, Moose and Roy drove off with the money.

Roy and Moose hadn't even opened the moneybag. Dennis had worked at a bank for a few years and told them that the money could be marked, could have exploding dye, or could have any of a thousand other booby traps, and that it would be best if he opened the bag. As a result both Roy and Moose were afraid to even peek inside, which was the biggest reason they were trying to get Dennis out of jail. The other being that

Dennis would expect it and wouldn't be pleased if they didn't.

The next day Roy called the Judge right after the trial ended for the day, while she was in her chambers.

"Hello?"

"Your Honor, it's your friendly kidnapper here. We need to make arrangements. That is if you wish to see your husband again."

"I see. Your buddy couldn't handle the matter, Roy?"

Dread filled Roy's body at the mention of his name. He swiftly pulled the phone away from his face, realizing Moose must have inadvertently mentioned his name. He slowly brought the phone back to his ear.

"We're talking about arrangements. And don't call me Roy."

"Okay, Roy. Talk."

"I expect you to declare Dennis Griner not guilty and set him free."

"How do I know my husband is alive, Roy?"

At that, Roy pulled a cassette player out of his pocket and was starting to turn it on when—

"And no recordings, Roy. If I can't ask him questions live, no deal. I want to talk to him now."

Roy shoved the recorder back into his pocket. "I can't let you talk to him. He's not here; he's not with me."

"I don't understand. Why not, Roy? If I can't know he's alive, we're done." The Judge hung up.

"Dang," Roy said as he pounded the dash. He had no choice. He needed to get the husband and Moose, bring them to town, and then call the Judge again.

When Chief Iris Evans and Detective Griffin arrived at the Judge's chambers, she asked them to take a seat. The Judge had asked Detective Griffin to come over with the chief. Iris and the Judge were best friends. They had been roommates in college and had gone to law school together, where Dashiell had been one of their professors. The Judge and Iris had similar personalities and sensibilities. They rarely had to explain to each other why they did something; the other one just knew why.

The Judge gave the kidnapping note to Iris, who read it and passed it on to Griffin. The Judge proceeded to tell them about the phone calls.

"So, Judge, the kidnappers: do they really have him?" Iris asked.

"They have Dashiell. They have no clue he is not my husband. They don't know he is your husband. The kidnappers must have been following me and assumed because Dashiell and I had been having lunch together that he was my husband. Chandler has been out of town on business; he's fine."

Iris turned the Coke bottle around and around in her hands while she thought. After a minute she said, "Judge, I guess you've got a plan."

"Yes, I do, but I'm not sure you and Griffin will like it."

"Go on."

"Judging by my phone conversations, I'd say the kidnappers are not professionals. One of them spilled the name of one of the other kidnappers—Roy. They seem to be bumblers. Considering Dennis Griner didn't use his gun during the robbery despite plenty of opportunities, I doubt they're prone to violence or that they intend to harm Dashiell. I expect he's being held out of town, which means they'll probably bring him into town when they call me. I expect they'll buy a burner phone at one of the Jiffy Marts on the west side of town, since the city is surrounded by water on the other three sides. That's where we'll catch them. We'll keep patrol cars out of the area, and the instant they call, we'll flood the west side with police cruisers. They'll get flustered, make some mistake, and we'll spot them."

Griffin spoke up as the Judge had expected. "That's a lot of assumptions. If any are wrong, that won't work."

"I agree with Griffin," Iris said. "What makes you think they'll get flustered?"

"I'll make sure of it."

"That's taking a big chance," Griffin said.

"I don't think so. They'll be disoriented; they won't know what to do. They'll make a mistake. Who knows? They might even let Dashiell go."

Iris chuckled while shaking her head and said, "I was just thinking, this serves Dashiell right. I'm sure you spent part of every lunch hour fending off his advances. If you just hadn't dated him before I did and spoiled him with those kisses."

Both Iris and the Judge laughed. Griffin shook his head. All three agreed to the plan, and Griffin left for headquarters to set things up.

Later that evening, Roy, Moose, and Dashiell pulled up to a Jiffy Mart on the west side of town. Moose went in and bought a burner phone. He came out, got into the van, and gave the phone to Roy, who dialed irritably.

"Hello?"

At that, Griffin, who was with the Judge, ordered the cruisers to flood the west side.

"Okay, I've got your husband right here. You can talk to him," Roy said as he put the phone into Dashiell's hand—he was blindfolded. Roy said, "Watch what you say."

"Hello," Dashiell said.

"What's your favorite newspaper?" the Judge asked.

"The Wall Street Journal."

"Give the phone back to the man."

Dashiell, unsure, slowly held out his hand.

Roy took the phone. "Okay, you happy now, Judge?"

"Yes, I am, Roy, very happy. That's not my husband." And she hung up.

Roy's mouth dropped open, and he dropped the phone. He got out of the van, walked around to the front, and beat on it with his fists.

At that moment, a police cruiser drove by. Within seconds lights were flashing, and the cruiser had the van boxed in while several other cruisers were swerving into the lot. Roy, the corners of his mouth turned up, a look of frustration on his face, plopped on the ground with his hands up. Moose got out of the van with his hands up too, glad it was over—but he'd never tell Roy that.

The End

15

British Shipping Clerk

I ran into Martin—who was with me on *that day* in 1925—at a tavern in London after I retired. It was 1963, my wife had passed away, and my children had moved to America for better opportunities they said. In 1925 Martin and I were both shipping clerks for the Ingram Shipping Line. I was assigned to the Hong Kong office, and he was working at the Bombay office in India. But the story starts three years earlier.

I had tempered my hopes of getting a job with Ingram in 1922, not wanting to be disappointed. My mother was optimistic. She said there was still a labor shortage because of all the lads killed during the Great War. Also, my grandfather had been an employee of the company and was well respected in spite of being a mere laborer. He always believed that a job bordered on the divine and treated his work as such. He never forgot a name or face. He seemed to know everyone in the company, and everyone, from the president on down, seemed to know him. I got the job and started work in the London office.

In 1923 I was unexpectedly asked to report to the Hong Kong office. Normally a person had to work five years before

being sent overseas; however, there had been an outbreak
of cholera in the Far East, and the office was short-handed.
The assignment was supposed to be for one year. Because
of the housing shortage in Hong Kong, I was put up in the
King James Hotel with my room and meals covered by the
company.

I worked all the time, because I was trying to live up to my
grandfather's reputation, and there were no employees my age
to socialize with. I wasn't charmed by the sensual offerings of
the Far East as others were. My grandfather had admonished
me regarding such matters with real stories of sadness and
ruin that he had witnessed over his lifetime.

Two years later I was still living at the King James. My
boss was supposed to send me back at the one-year mark but
conveniently never got around to it. London never questioned
the continuing expenses from the King James.

In 1925 due to a labor shortage in the Bombay office, I was
assigned there for three months. I barely stayed three days.
Martin, who was not much older than I, had been assigned
to look after me when I arrived. We met at the dock upon my
arrival in India and promptly caught a train to a mountain
resort. Martin explained that the office was being moved, and
employees had the week off. And if I liked skiing, there was
snow on the ground. I wasn't interested in going to the resort,
but it appeared to be something Martin did often. Not knowing where else to go, I went. After we arrived and checked into
the hotel, Martin gave me an address.

"What's this for?"

"I have an errand to run and might not be back for a while.
And they'll take care of you."

"Take care of me how?" I wondered.

Martin grinned, raising and lowering his eyebrows rapidly.

I stayed in my hotel room.

The next morning Martin headed out again and told me to meet him at a specific restaurant at noon. I decided to walk around the town until then. The town catered to the well-to-do: nicely dressed men and women everywhere and lots of specialty shops and lots of British and other foreigners. I wanted to see the train depot again. It was built like a smaller version of the Parthenon, and with the light reflecting off the snow, the scene was enhanced. The train tracks ended at the station as it was the last stop on the line. The town was surrounded by mountains on three sides. If you stood at the depot and looked down the narrow valley, the tracks went straight for miles as they descended to the plain below.

I decided to peruse the shops in town. In one of the shop windows, I saw a statue of Venus, just like the one my grandfather had given my mother, so I went in. Standing at the counter was a most beautiful young lady wearing a formal, but not extravagant, white dress. She reminded me of a porcelain doll.

"Excuse me, what's your name?" I was looking forward to chin-wagging with a young British woman; it had been a while.

"Dhara."

"Dhara. That's an Indian name, but you look so . . . so British."

"My mother was British, and my father is half British and half Indian."

"You live here, in India?"

"Yes, my father says you cannot go through life being half and half; you must choose one or the other. And since my mother has passed away, he decided on Indian."

"What about you? What do you want?"

"Since I'm fourteen, my father decides such things."

"Fourteen? You can't . . . I mean you're so . . . ah . . . mature looking."

Dhara blushed. I could tell I did too, because my face felt warm.

"Can I help you find something in the shop?"

"Yes, I'd like to look at the Venus statue in the front window, please."

"Certainly. Follow me."

We walked to the front window. She had brought a step stool so she could reach the statue. As she reached into the case, she lost her balance, and the stool tipped over. I grabbed her around the waist and pulled her to me to keep her from falling. Her feet were dangling off the floor as I held her body against mine. As I loosened my grip, her body slowly slid down my body. For a few moments, we both stood there, my arms wrapped around her and hers around me. Our bodies pressed against each other as we looked into each other's eyes.

"Dhara," a loud threatening voice bellowed from the rear of the shop.

At that, we let go of each other. Dhara headed back to the counter, and I was out the door. I could imagine what the man, her father I assumed, was thinking. Even under the most appropriate circumstances, a man and woman touching in public is scandalous in India. My step quickened as I headed down the street. I didn't look back as I heard the shopkeeper shouting in a language I didn't understand.

I arrived at the restaurant a few minutes before noon. Martin came along, slapped me on the shoulder, and said, "Let's eat."

The place was busy and served all manner of food. Martin and I were sitting across from each other at a table to ourselves.

We were almost finished when I saw a commotion by the

kitchen door. The restaurant's proprietor, Dhara's father, Dhara, and a policeman were having a heated exchange as arms flailed. Martin heard the commotion and turned around to see what was going on.

Then Dhara's father pointed directly at me while shouting to the policeman. Martin watched and listened. He turned back around and said, "We've got to get out of here now. On the count of three, we need to run."

"Wait. Run? What for?"

Martin understood the language—I didn't—and said, "The man is telling the police that you took advantage of his daughter."

"What, but that . . . that's not right."

"It doesn't matter. This is a battle you can't win. We'll split up outside and meet at the train station."

Martin jumped up and ran, and so did I. That's what happens when you're caught up in the moment, letting your emotions get the better of you: you run. I did have the wherewithal to throw a pound note on the table. I certainly didn't need to be accused of stealing.

Martin was out the door, and I followed close behind. We ran in opposite directions. Unknown to me, outside the restaurant stood a newspaper photographer, silently watching.

When I got to the train station, I was out of breath. A train was starting to leave the station. Although I didn't see any police, I heard police whistles in the distance. I ran into the station and then back out after not seeing Martin. I ran over to one side of the tracks and saw a sled propped up against what appeared to be a maintenance shed. I ran over, put the sled on the ground, and pushed off. I was heading down the valley passing the train when I lost control of the sled and smashed into a tree. At least that's what the doctor and his wife told me, and I had no reason to doubt them.

The British doctor and his wife, who were on the train, had seen me crash and pulled the emergency cord. They rushed off the train and had the porters bring me into their compartment. I came to a short time later. I told them what happened in the shop, the events at the restaurant, and my taking the sled. Since I hadn't done anything wrong, except perhaps borrowing the sled, I didn't see any problem with telling the truth.

"Well, young man," said the doctor, "you do need to be more careful. It's so easy to have a misunderstanding with strangers, much less with foreigners."

"I have to agree with you."

"Listen, come to the dining car with Mrs. Rattle and me. I know you've eaten, but it would be good if you could eat and drink something. With that nasty bump on your head, we should keep an eye on you for a while."

"Okay." Since we wouldn't get to Bombay until lunchtime the following day, the Rattles were kind enough to buy me a seat in a compartment I shared with five others. The doctor let me know there would be an hour stop at Musa in the morning. I slept through that hour. After the stop, the doctor and his wife came by and asked that I join them for breakfast in the dining car, which I was glad to do.

After we ordered, the doctor said, "Well, Edward, I have some unfortunate news for you." He unfolded a newspaper and pushed it to my side of the table.

I couldn't believe it. On the front page was a photo of me running with a policeman, Dhara's father, and Dhara chasing after me. I looked up at the doctor and his wife in disbelief. I looked back down and read the story. There was my name. I was thankful Martin wasn't mentioned.

The article stated that Dhara's father was a prominent, wealthy shopkeeper and emphasized that his daughter was fourteen. It didn't explicitly indicate what I had done, but it gave the impression I had taken advantage of the girl.

When we got to Bombay, I thanked the doctor and his wife for helping me, and they wished me the best. It took me a few hours, but I was finally able to track down the boss of the Bombay office, Mr. Anderson. When I went to his makeshift office, I saw a copy of the newspaper on his desk. He told me that a ship, the *Anna Mareu*, was leaving for Hong Kong in three hours, the captain was expecting me, and I needed to be on it.

"Back to Hong Kong? Let me explain what happened, Mr. Anderson."

But he cut me off. "Son, it doesn't matter. I don't need this kind of publicity. You need to go."

Several days later I was in Hong Kong. And several days after that, I was shipped off to London. The story was in British newspapers around the world. I guess it had been a slow news day.

When I got to London, the boss told me to take two weeks off.

My parents never brought up the incident, and by then it seemed like sour grapes if I tried to explain.

The first time I was alone with my grandfather, he chuckled. "Edward, you don't need to explain. There's clearly more to the story. You, unfortunately, were in the wrong place at the wrong time. The best thing you can do is forget it."

You usually got a promotion after you returned to London from an overseas assignment. I didn't, not that year nor the next. I decided to see Mr. Wilson, the personnel director, and ask him why.

"Sit down, young man. What can I do for you?" Mr. Wilson said.

"Mr. Wilson, sir, I have not received a promotion since I returned from my assignment in Hong Kong in 1925. And I've always gotten good performance reviews."

"Well, Edward, the shipping business is tough now, very competitive. And as the president of the company says, we have to watch every pence. There are a lot of young men out of work, so the environment is not conducive to increasing wages."

"Is there anything I can do?"

"Yes, yes, keep up the good work."

At that, I left his office. His answers were dismissive. He didn't pull my file, he didn't know the first thing about me, and I knew plenty of others who had gotten promotions, most of whom were not as diligent as I was. I decided to pursue the matter through someone else. But whom? The next time I saw my grandfather, I asked for his help.

"Grandfather, I want your help with a career matter for *a friend* who also works at Ingram."

"Certainly, Edward, you know I'm always willing to offer advice."

"Suppose someone at Ingram kept getting passed over for a promotion and wanted to know why. Who would this employee talk to if the normal channels of inquiry yielded no information? This employee is not looking to use influence but looking for information."

"I see. So Mr. Wilson has been useless. Knowing Mr. Wilson, I can understand that. The best person for your friend to speak with is someone on the promotion board. I'm not sure who is currently on the board, but I'll find out."

I didn't see my grandfather for several weeks, but when I did, the following transpired: "Edward, I have some information concerning your friend's lack of promotions. I found out that your friend's personnel file has never gotten to the promotion board for review, which shouldn't happen. Anyone whose performance is average or better is supposed to get reviewed. The individual charged with getting the personnel files to the board is Mr. Harrison. Oh yes, Mr. Harrison is the brother-in-law of Mr. Anderson, the head of the Bombay office. Two weeks before the promotion board's annual meeting, which is public knowledge, your friend needs to go to his boss and ask him to send his personnel file directly to one of the members of the promotion board. It doesn't matter which member. The boss shouldn't give it a second thought because it's not unusual for an employee to make this request, and the file will not go through Mr. Harrison."

All I could say was thank you to my grandfather knowing that he had figured out I was the *friend*.

After the next promotion board meeting, I was promoted, and so was Mr. Anderson. He was now my boss in London. I wasn't to get another promotion while at Ingram.

The first few years after returning from Hong Kong, I had difficulty getting a date. I thought it was something about me. What else could it be. I always assumed the worst. I finally asked a young woman with whom I was enamored.

"Lorraine, will you ever go out with me?"

"No."

"Why not?"

"Well, Edward, you're nice and all, but none of us women believe you'll be a good provider. Everyone your age has had two or three promotions," she said bluntly.

Lorraine was right. My wage was barely enough for me to live on. Fortunately, what I loved most was reading, and I could read for free at the library. Often, after work and on weekends, I would spend my time there. The library wasn't cramped and was well lit, unlike my apartment. I got to know the staff quite well.

At the time, Lorraine's comment shook me, but I still wanted to get married someday. Eventually, a few years later, I married Bertha, who was five years my senior and an orphan. We met, or I should say, she met me at the library. One of the librarians told me that a woman who was a frequent library patron had inquired about me. Several days later, that woman stopped by my table to chat.

"Excuse me, my name is Bertha. I wondered if you'd join me for lunch at the Wellington, down the street, for some fish and chips?"

I was startled by a woman asking me out, yet it was something I had dreamed of. When it happened though, I wasn't sure I liked it, but I couldn't think of a reason to say no.

"Yes, my name is—"

"Edward Murdock. Yes, I know," Bertha replied matter-of-factly.

Bertha wasn't unattractive, and I wasn't in love with her. I liked her, but by then I had given up on meeting someone; I said yes when she asked me to marry her. She was nice to me, worked hard, and never complained, ever. And later, no doubt, she saved my life.

It happened one night in bed. I told her I was considering joining the republican forces in Spain to fight Franco and the fascists.

"Why?" Bertha asked.

"Because it's a just cause. It's the noble thing to do."

"Living an ethical life is a noble thing. War's not noble, and it's certainly not for the men fighting. You'll be in trenches for months at a time, in mud and muck, littered with body parts and human excrement. You'll be lucky to get one meal a day, and you'll go without sleep for days at a time. The first winter you're there will turn out to be the coldest in the past one hundred years, and you'll have to relieve yourself in your clothes for days on end."

"My God, how do you know that?"

"I've read a lot about the Great War."

"Why would you want to read about that?"

"I want to know about things that men don't let women do."

That did it for me. I had terrible dreams on and off for the next few weeks and decided perhaps I was leading a noble enough life.

That conversation also changed the way I thought of Bertha. After that, I was curious about what she knew, what she thought, what books she was reading, and why. Each week I made sure we had time for discussions.

I had thought of a woman only as a domestic homemaker. Instead of having settled for Bertha, I realized I had found a gem. Our talks were treasures. Even though she left school at the age of ten, I knew few people with her knowledge and ability to think.

"I see you're reading *On the Origin of Species* by Charles Darwin," I said one day.

"Yes, I am."

"Isn't that about evolution?"

"Yes."

"Do you believe in this evolution?"

"Well, Darwin may be correct about evolution, but the idea's not new. Mr. Darwin's grandfather Erasmus was a proponent of evolution, and the idea has been around since the ancient Greeks. Lucretius, a Roman poet, wrote about it more than two thousand years ago."

"Oh."

"Yes, but Darwin's theory about natural selection survival of the fittest is poppycock."

"Poppycock?"

"Absolutely. Darwin said that nature was always improving species, daily, even hourly, to provide for the selection of the fittest. But what mechanism does that? What's controlling it? Nature only requires a species live long enough to reproduce. Nature abhors change in a species that's surviving. The degree to which the species is surviving is irrelevant. The problem is Darwin had spent part of his life around breeders, so he transferred this idea—humans improving animals by selective breeding—to nature. Even some of the biologists Darwin worked with told him he was wrong, that there was not a sliver of evidence for this. But Darwin had been put on such a pedestal by the scientific community that his words— all of them—were treated as gospel."

This type of conversation with Bertha continued for years.

Here's another time. "I see you're reading a book on Mark Twain," I said.

"Yes, I adore him. He's full of it."

"Full of it?"

"Wit."

Eventually, on occasion, we would celebrate certain days during the year that Bertha picked out. When these days popped up, they were always a surprise to me. I remember the first time it happened. It was Friday, April 21, 1944, and I had just gotten home from work.

"Edward," Bertha greeted me at the door dressed to go out. "I have saved up enough for us go to the Wellington for fish and chips."

"What's the occasion?"

"The Provisional Government of France in Algiers announced the right of French women to vote."

October 7, 1952, a Tuesday, was the most unusual day we ever celebrated, at least to me. That was the date Joseph Woodland and Bernard Silver were granted a patent on something called a barcode. I didn't have a clue what a barcode was. Bertha said the railroads were using it to keep track of railcars and that it would be a big thing one day.

I had been going to the library for years, and it had been instrumental in my finding a wife. As it turned out, it also led to a new job and improved financial prospects. Several years after our marriage, I was sitting in the library when I was approached by someone.

"Excuse me, Mr. Murdock, Mr. Edward Murdock?" a gentleman said as he held out his hand.

"Yes," I said as I reached to shake his hand. He was well dressed. A man of stature, I supposed.

"I am Mr. Hardwick, Mr. George Hardwick," he said as he handed me his card. "I'm managing editor of the *London Post-Dispatch*. If you could come to my office this Saturday for a job interview at nine a.m., I would be most grateful."

Noticing the expression of surprise on my face, Mr. Hardwick asked if he could sit down and explain.

"Mr. Murdock, my paper needs a newspaperman, a reporter, here in London. The hours occasionally will be erratic with some travel outside London but none outside England. The salary is fifty percent more than your current earnings with a possible twenty-five percent increase after one year of service. I have excellent reports about your work from inquiries I have made at the Ingram Shipping Line. And having seen you in the library often, I have inquired of the staff about your areas of study, which I am told include writing and grammar. Also, I admit a certain degree of prejudice on my part for wanting to hire you.

"In 1899 I was a young dockworker for Ingram. At a labor union rally, some of the more radical members called for a work slowdown since it was technically illegal to strike. Being new, young, and perhaps naive, I jumped up and yelled, 'No! We either work or not, but we don't mess with the job.' After the meeting a couple of ruffians began pummeling me. Your grandfather saw this and ran them off. I heard several days later that the word had been passed around that I was under his protection. I don't have to tell you how much respect your grandfather commanded at Ingram from both the most radical to the most conservative employee. No one bothered me again."

I got the job with the *London Post-Dispatch,* and Bertha and my financial situation improved considerably. To me, there was a sense of irony. For decades my financial situation had stagnated because of a newspaper, and now my financial situation improved because of a newspaper.

So there I was in 1963, and I had run into Martin. It was pleasant running into someone I knew, albeit slightly, from Ingram. I had not seen Martin since that day in 1925. I had read about him here and there in the Ingram newsletter. He had been the head of the Cape Town office for many years before he retired. One thing I do remember about Martin even after all this time is that he liked to talk.

"Oh, by the way, I've never had a chance to tell you," Martin said "Remember that day in India in the restaurant when we ran from that Indian man and the policeman? They were after me."

The End

16

I Shouldn't Have

I shouldn't have answered the door with boiled okra in my mouth. But the salesman made a mistake too. He didn't count on Martha, my wife. And you shouldn't make assumptions about Martha: you'd be wrong, way wrong.

Martha is a fine woman, as fine as you can find these days. That she is a smart woman you can tell with one gander. Conniving some folks say, not me. Just smarter than most, in spite of not finishing high school. Martha's maxim is schooling doesn't make you smart—books and life do. That's why she works at the library; she gets plenty of both there.

She wore a light-yellow dress to her knees and no shoes. It was a dress she wore on days she worked part-time at the library. She didn't wear shoes much in the house. And for stockings, she wears the old-fashioned kind with garters—you need to know that.

It was Tuesday. I know because that's my long workday. Ten hours packing boxes and loading the semi-trailers that have been sitting in the South Georgia sun. When I get home on Tuesdays, my clothes are completely soaked through. All I want to do is take a shower, eat supper, and go to bed. No reading, writing, lovemaking, or salesmen for that matter. I bet he, the salesman, knew it was my long day at the factory. Thought I'd be an easy mark.

After my shower, the five of us sat down for supper—Martha, Jack, Jason, Timmy, and me. The kids know they can get the best of me on Tuesdays. They misbehave and parlay with each other around the supper table while I'm trying to eat. Tired as I am, I leave 'em be.

I skewered food with my fork, not paying attention to what was on the plate. Martha was splitting her time between eating and taming the wild bunch. She didn't notice when the doorbell rang.

Wanting a reprieve from the hoopla, I answered the door. I hadn't noticed that Martha had put a few pieces of boiled okra on my plate. She knows better. She knows I hate boiled okra. I can't swallow the stuff. It's too slimy. I had put a piece in my mouth and hadn't realized it until I was opening the door. It was too late; I had to leave it there.

"Okra is good for you. You should have some now and again even if you don't like it. We all have to do stuff we don't like sometimes." I don't like the grin on Martha's face when she says those things. Kinda like there's something behind it. Like there's more to it, and she isn't going to tell. Sometimes it's hard to tell if a woman is flirting, being catty, or not giving you any thought at all.

There he was, the salesman, with a silver-black vacuum cleaner. I invited him in. Because of Martha's family history, I have to invite salesmen in. Martha's father was a successful Fuller Brush man and her mother too, a Fuller Brush woman, actually. In fact, her mother usually outsold her father. Martha always makes a big point of that. Because of this rule—inviting salesmen in—we do own a few things we shouldn't, like the hundred-dollar steak knives. Martha and I remember that evening differently, so I don't bring it up.

When I saw the salesman with the vacuum cleaner, I had three thoughts. First, I would be inviting him in. Second, our vacuum cleaner was busted. That could be my fault—I don't think so though. As I told Martha, how was I to know that Timmy would use the vacuum cleaner to pick up his toys when I told him to clean up his room. Shows ingenuity Martha said. And the third thought, the okra would be in my mouth for a while.

We went into the den. We're not pretentious folks; we don't have a living room. In the South, only rich folks, or at least the well-to-do, have living rooms. You know, the room that gets all the best furniture and never, okay almost never, gets used. The salesman sat down on the sofa. I sat down in a chair. Of course, there was noise coming from the kitchen— kids shouting, plates banging, Martha saying, "Settle down." The salesman pretended not to notice. That's one thing you can count on from salesmen; they're polite.

He told me the specifications of the vacuum, but I didn't hear him. I was distracted by his shirt and tie. He was wearing a plaid shirt. He was also wearing a plaid tie, but it was a different color and pattern of plaid. That's not right, I thought. That's against the rules; Martha told me so. She told me you couldn't wear a plaid tie with a plaid shirt if it was different plaid. And it sure didn't look right; I'll say that.

I wanted to excuse myself and tell the salesman I needed to use the bathroom. The okra was getting slimier, and I needed to get rid of it, and the plaid clash was making me dizzy. But my momma taught me it was rude to excuse yourself when you had company. You might never see them again, and you needed to give a good account of yourself. And I needed to make a good impression to make up for the noises from the kitchen.

I thought maybe it'd be best to go ahead and buy the vacuum cleaner. We needed one after all.

"Okay, you sold me. I'll take it," I mumbled. "How much?"

"Great," the salesman said. "It's a thousand dollars."

"A thousand dollars!" I exclaimed in disbelief, the okra almost slipping from my mouth.

"Yes, but let me show you what it can do," he said with a great big smile.

He probably realized later he should have stopped there and had me sign the papers. And I would have too. But before I could utter another word, he dumped a small bag of dirt on the carpet and was grinding the dirt into the carpet with his shoe. Then he plugged it in—the vacuum, not his shoe—and started vacuuming. When he finished, he pulled out the vacuum cleaner bag and showed me all the dirt. And I'm thinking, uh-huh.

As if the okra, the plaid shirt, and the plaid tie weren't enough, now the thousand dollars was swirling in my head.

The kids burst through the door on their way to their rooms with Martha chasing behind them. As she passed me, I said, "Hon, this salesman is selling vacuum cleaners."

"That's nice," she said as she continued chasing the boys up to their rooms.

I felt as if I were standing on the gallows, nowhere to go, with a slimy piece of boiled okra in my mouth, and the hanging judge had run out before giving the nod to the executioner. I wanted this to be over.

The agreement to purchase the vacuum cleaner was laid out on the coffee table next to the credit agreement. I walked to the coffee table, got on my knees, and was about to sign the agreements when Martha walked in.

"Can I see it first, dear?" she said.

I put down the pen and said, "Sure," the best I could with slimy okra in my mouth.

The smile stayed on the salesman's face as if it were glued. He pulled out another bag of dirt.

With my hand covering my mouth, I pleaded, "Oh please, don't do that. Just tell her how much it is: a thousand dollars. I'll vouch for the fact that you already dumped a bag of dirt on the carpet and vacuumed it up. And that this is the best vacuum in the county, maybe even the state."

There was no change in Martha's expression, but I could tell, just felt it, that she was thinking.

"Dusty," she said. I didn't know the salesman's name was Dusty, but there it was right on his name tag. Martha says I'm not paying attention half the time. "You saw my boys, and Jack, the oldest, needs braces. The dentist doesn't give credit; we have to pay in cash. You don't want my boy to go without braces, do you?" I noticed Martha called them *my* boys, not *our* boys.

"No, madam, certainly not," Dusty said his smile faltering.

Then Martha reached under the hem of her dress and started pulling one stocking off.

"Ah...what are you doing?" Dusty asked, pulling at his collar as if it were too tight.

Martha said, "Well, I need to know if the carpet *is* clean where you dumped the dirt, and the best way to tell is to lie on the carpet with Harold on top of me, if you get my meaning," as the other stocking came off.

What the heck? *This* had never happened before. My mouth was agape even with the okra. After the other stocking came off, Martha's hands were at the zipper on the back of her dress. I've never seen a salesman, or anyone, come to think of it, move so fast. He grabbed the vacuum cleaner and whizzed past Martha. As he passed her, her dress crumpled to the floor. He was running by then. I heard the front door slam as Martha's bra landed beside her dress. I heard more running, a car door slamming, and a car leaving. I was trying to figure out what had just happened. Martha sure thinks quicker than me, quicker than anyone I know.

"Ah Lawd have mercy," I said.

"Sweetie," she said, "do come here. I want to check if the carpet is clean, even if it's Tuesday."

I don't know what happened to the okra. It was gone.

The End

CPSIA information can be obtained
at www.ICGtesting.com
Printed in the USA
JSHW031919151122
33212JS00001B/65